Best

SWIMMING WITH DOLPHINS
TRACKING GORILLAS

How to have the world's best wildlife encounters

IAN WOOD

Bradt

First published August 2012

Bradt Travel Guides Ltd, IDC House, The Vale, Chalfont St Peter, Bucks SL9 9RZ, England
www.bradtguides.com
Published in the USA by The Globe Pequot Press Inc, PO Box 480, Guilford, Connecticut 06437-0480

ISBN-13: 978 1 84162 404 4

BRITISH LIBRARY CATALOGUING IN PUBLICATION DATA
A catalogue record for this book is available from the British Library

PHOTOGRAPHS
Front cover: *Top* Pod of Hawaiian spinner dolphins *Stenella longirostris* (Yukihiro Fukuda/NHPA)
Bottom Mountain gorilla silverback *Gorilla beringei beringei*, Virunga Mountains, Rwanda (Andy Rouse/NHPA)
Back cover: *Top* Observing lions *Panthera leo* on a walking safari, Luangwa Valley, Zambia (Frans Lanting/FLPA)
Bottom Emperor penguins *Aptenodytes forsteri*, Weddell Sea, Antarctica (Bernard Breton/Dreamstime.com)
Spine: Bengal tiger *Panthera tigris tigris*, Ranthambore Tiger Reserve, India (Aditya Singh/Imagebroker/FLPA)
Title page: Giant panda cub *Ailuropoda melanoleuca*, Sichuan Province, China (Photo Researchers/FLPA)

Text See page 180

DESIGNER Pepi Bluck
IMAGE RESEARCH Pepi Bluck

Production managed by Jellyfish Print Solutions; printed and bound in India

FOREWORD

JONATHAN & ANGELA SCOTT

Sitting in our safari vehicle surrounded by lions in the Maasai Mara in Kenya is as close to paradise as Angie and I could hope for – seeking out encounters with wild animals has shaped our lives. Hardly surprising, then, that my first response when I opened Ian Wood's thoughtful and informative book was to dust off my rucksack, fill it with cameras and lenses, and head into the wild. Colourful images of lions, bears, penguins, dolphins and many other creatures made me realise how incredibly fortunate Angie and I have been in exploring wild places and getting to know their charismatic inhabitants.

At the same time, we are acutely aware of the impact that wildlife-based tourism can have – for better and for worse. Kenya's thriving travel industry generates much-needed foreign exchange for the country, helping to conserve its national parks and reserves. But without careful planning tourism can easily show its destructive side, threatening the wellbeing of the very environment that sustains it.

I like to think of myself as an optimist – someone who finds resonance with the phrase 'better to light a candle than to curse the darkness'; someone who believes that there is still time for us humans to come to our senses and reconnect with this extraordinarily beautiful planet of ours and treat it with the respect it deserves. So it is alarming to witness the speed at which the last remnants of our natural world are disappearing. That is why we need books like *Swimming with Dolphins, Tracking Gorillas*. They encourage us to be adventurous in our travels while treading lightly along the way. Ian Wood reveals how to experience magical animal encounters that for most of us are the stuff of dreams. The delight of rounding a corner along a sandy track in India's Kanha National Park to find a tiger lying in the dappled shade of a tree or chancing upon a leopard gambolling about with her cub among the rocky hideaways of the Maasai Mara come easily to mind from our own scrapbook of memories.

Travel to far-off places can be both exciting and affordable. The challenge is in knowing where to start and when to travel. In this instance you can sit back and relax – Ian Wood has done the hard graft for you. I particularly loved the Calendar section that clearly indicates the best months to see the animals Ian features, each colour-coded and organised into ecozones alongside a tantalising array of encounter highlights pinpointing exact locations. Planning your next wildlife adventure has never been easier.

Jonathan and Angela Scott are award-winning authors and photographers known worldwide for their contribution to the BBC's *Big Cat Diary*. They are also the photographers and co-authors of Bradt's acclaimed book *The Marsh Lions* (www.bradtguides.com).

CONTENTS

WILDLIFE CALENDAR

	PAGE	JAN	FEB	MAR	APR	MAY	JUN	JUL	AUG	SEP	OCT	NOV	DEC
Alligators	126	●	●	●	●	●	●	●	●	●	●	●	●
Brown bears, Eurasian	50				●	●	●	●	●	●			
Cheetahs	68	●	●	●	●	●	●	●	●	●	●	●	●
Chimpanzees	22	●	●	●	●	●	●	●	●	●	●	●	●
Condors & vultures	106	●	●	●	●	●	●	●	●	●	●	●	●
Dolphins	136	●	●	●	●	●	●	●	●	●	●	●	●
Elephants	78	●	●	●	●	●	●	●	●	●	●	●	●
Galápagos	152	●	●	●	●	●	●	●	●	●	●	●	●
Giant panda	100		●	●	●							●	
Gorillas	16	●	●	●	●	●	●	●	●	●	●	●	●
Grizzly bears	46						●	●	●	●			
Hippos	122	●	●	●	●	●	●	●	●	●	●	●	●
Komodo dragons	54	●	●	●	●	●	●	●	●	●	●	●	●
Lemurs	36				●	●				●	●	●	●
Leopards	74	●	●	●	●	●	●	●	●	●	●	●	●
Lions	64	●	●	●	●	●	●	●	●	●	●	●	●
Macaws	58						●	●	●	●	●	●	●
Manta rays	170	●	●	●	●	●	●	●	●	●	●	●	●
Orangutans	28	●	●	●	●	●	●	●	●	●	●	●	●
Penguins	116	●	●	●								●	●
Polar bears	110						●	●	●	●	●		
Proboscis monkeys	40	●	●	●	●	●	●	●	●	●	●	●	●
Puffins	174				●	●	●	●					
Rhinos	88	●	●	●	●	●	●	●	●	●	●	●	●
Seals & sea lions	148	●	●	●	●	●	●	●	●	●	●	●	●
Sharks	162	●	●	●	●	●	●	●	●	●	●	●	●
Shoebills	132	●	●	●	●	●	●	●	●	●	●	●	●
Snow leopards	92		●	●									
Tigers	10	●	●	●	●						●	●	●
Turtles	158	●	●	●	●	●	●	●	●	●	●	●	●
Wildebeest migration	84	●	●	●	●	●	●	●	●	●	●	●	●
Whale sharks	166	●	●	●	●	●	●	●	●	●	●	●	●
Whales	142	●	●	●	●	●	●	●	●	●	●	●	●
Wolves	96	●	●	●	●	●	●	●	●	●	●	●	●

ENCOUNTER HIGHLIGHTS

JANUARY

- Swim with **whale sharks**, Tofo, Mozambique
- Track **mountain gorillas**, Uganda & Rwanda
- **Wildebeest** calve in southern Serengeti, Tanzania
- Swim with **humpback whales**, Dominican Republic
- **Wolf** tracking, Yellowstone National Park, USA

FEBRUARY

- **Wolf** tracking, Romania
- **Penguin** chicks fledge, Antarctica
- End of dry season, Indian **tiger** reserves
- Dive among **bull & tiger sharks**, Bahamas
- Swim with **sea lions & dolphins**, Port Phillip Bay, Australia

MARCH

- Mount an expedition in search of **snow leopards**, Ladkah, India
- Dive with **hammerhead sharks**, Layang-layang, Malaysia
- Watch for **hippos**, Luangwa National Park, Zambia
- Track **lowland gorillas**, Lopé National Park, Gabon
- Snorkel on a **coral reef**, Port Launay Marine NP, Seychelles

APRIL

- Seek out the **giant panda**, China
- Swim with **whale sharks**, Ningaloo Reef, Australia
- Courtship of waved albatrosses, Española, **Galápagos** Islands
- Boat along a river to see **proboscis monkeys**, Borneo
- Ringtail **lemurs** 'stink fight' for mating rights, Madagascar

MAY

- Watch **Eurasian brown bears** from a hide, Finland
- Seek out howler monkeys in the **Costa Rican rainforest**
- Track **chimpanzees**, Tanzania
- **Puffins** return to nest, Skomer Island, UK
- Search for the **shoebill**, Bangweulu Swamps, Zambia

JUNE

- Swimming with **dolphins**, Azores
- Track **lion, cheetah & leopard**, Zambia
- Track **rhino** on foot, Damaraland, Namibia
- **Horseriding safari**, Botswana
- Cage diving with **great white sharks**, South Africa

JULY

- Watch **grizzly bears** catching salmon, Canada
- Snorkel with **humpback whales**, Tonga, French Polynesia
- **Wildebeest migration**, Tanzania/Kenya
- Explore the **Pantanal** in search of jaguars, Brazil
- Track **elephants**, Mana Pools National Park, Zimbabwe

AUGUST

- Swim with **beluga whales**, Hudson Bay, Canada
- Dive with **turtles**, Sipadan, Malaysia
- Watch **macaws** at salt licks, Peru
- See giant tortoises in Santa Cruz, **Galápagos** Islands
- Cruise Svalbard, Norway, in search of **polar bears**

SEPTEMBER

- Dive with **seals**, Farne Islands, UK
- Track **komodo dragons**, Indonesia
- Hike in search of **lammergeiers**, Ordesa National Park, Spain
- Encounter **orangutans** in Borneo & Sumatra
- Track **elephants** on foot, Okavango Delta, Botswana

OCTOBER

- Start of **tiger**-viewing season, India
- Swim with **dolphins**, Bay of Plenty, New Zealand
- **Seals**, Farne Islands, UK
- Watch **condors** rise on morning thermals, Colca Canyon, Peru
- Birth of baby **lemurs**, Madagascar

NOVEMBER

- Swim with **killer whales**, Norway
- Dive with **hammerhead sharks**, Socorro Islands, Mexico
- Observe an **emperor penguin** colony, Antarctica
- Track **lowland gorillas**, Dzanga-Ndoki National Park, CAR
- Kayak with **alligators**, Everglades, USA

DECEMBER

- Swim with **manta rays**, Yap, Micronesia
- 4x4 encounters with **Ethiopian wolves**, Bale Mountains
- Start of green turtle mating season, **Galápagos** Islands
- Swim with **dolphins**, Pemba, Mozambique
- Kayak with **penguins**, Antarctica

IAN WOOD is a writer and photographer who specialises in wildlife, travel and nature. Not that his journey has been orthodox. For 18 years he toured the world as half of the internationally acclaimed comedy act, *The Invisible Men*, performing in over 40 countries across five continents. But spare time was spent in search of wildlife, indulging a particular passion for rainforests and oceans. Over the last four years his articles and photographs have been published in a variety of newspapers and magazines including *The Daily Telegraph* and *nationalgeographic.com*. In partnership with The Orangutan Foundation he also runs a number of photographic tours to Borneo which raise money for their conservation efforts. For more information please visit his website, www.agoodplace.co.uk.

ACKNOWLEDGEMENTS

First I would like to thank Adrian Phillips and all the Bradt team for making this book possible. I'm forever indebted to my project manager and editor, Tricia Hayne, for her undying support, editorial expertise, humour and friendship. In fact, without Tricia this book would be a random collection of wildlife encounters spread across a bewildering array of files and folders on my computer!

I'm extremely grateful to the various tour operators who helped me clarify the best places and times to see such a range of wildlife. In particular, Chris McIntyre at Expert Africa, Derek Schuurman and Dianne Ceresa at Rainbow Tours, Chris Breen at Wildlife Worldwide, Teresa Bennett at Dive Worldwide, and Will Bolsover at Natural World Safaris consistently went beyond the call of duty. Paul Goldstein from Exodus also helped, not just in providing photos but also with information on polar bears.

Travelling the world in search of wildlife is not the cheapest of passions and I've been genuinely overwhelmed by the support I've received during the last few years. Brenda Franck and Calvin Brummer at Pemba Dive, Noleen Withers at Somente Aqua, Mary Jo and Louis Van Aardt at Kizingo Lodge and Mahmud Bangkaru all contributed with acts of generosity for which I'm eternally indebted. Photographing wildlife in Borneo over the last few years would never have been possible without my guide and friend Edy Aja, and Ashley Leiman from the Orangutan Foundation has always been a source of inspiration.

Mike Unwin, whose work has been an inspiration to me and many other wildlife lovers, wrote the Pantanal section and contributed material on polar bears, lammergeiers and beluga whales.

Last but certainly not least there's my personal back-up team. Huge thanks to my wife Jo for her love, support and mutual fascination with the natural world. To my children, Scott and Renee, for their understanding when I disappear for weeks on end, and to my grandson, Leon, who has already made me promise to take him to the rainforest when he's older. There you go, Leon; it's in writing now.

INTRODUCTION

❝ *The love for all living creatures is the most noble attribute of man.* ❞

CHARLES DARWIN

Several years ago, snorkelling off the coast of Mozambique, I heard the unmistakable sound of clicks and squeaks. Seconds later – emerging from the blue – a pod of dolphins appeared, swimming towards me at high speed before veering off and streaking away. But then they returned. Slower this time, spinning round, turning on their sides, exchanging eye contact from barely a metre away. An inspiring encounter with wild animals – on their terms.

But shouldn't all wildlife experiences be like this? Whether it's tracking mountain gorillas, walking in search of elephants or diving with sharks, the fundamental rules remain the same. As humans, we are merely temporary guests in their environment –privileged to glimpse their world. And so the idea for this book grew, to pull together the world's best wildlife experiences. Sadly there have been a few casualties; the initial list was too long for the realities of publishing and several species failed to make the final line up. Particular apologies must go to meerkats, basking sharks and wild dogs.

Each encounter features other wildlife that you are likely to see along the way. Walking through African savanna in search of lions is thrilling – but it's also an opportunity to observe smaller creatures such as antlions lurking in the sand. The lure of tigers might inspire you to visit India, but sloth bears are a great added bonus. And while macaws are the main attraction at a salt lick, keep half an eye out for giant otters swimming in the river.

Wherever possible I've included information that will help you to make your wildlife quest as positive as possible. For example, photos that you take of cheetahs or whale sharks can be uploaded to a database, leading to a better understanding of these animals. A selection of hand-picked tour operators is also listed for each encounter, based on the criteria of specialist knowledge and a willingness to engage in conservation.

No matter how well prepared you are, there can never be any guarantees with wildlife. Yet whether you are sitting in a hide waiting for a glimpse of a bear, or searching the trees along a river for signs of proboscis monkeys, or staring into the blue for that elusive whale shark: all can bring a heightened sense of awareness that comes from immersing yourself in the natural world. Travel is always more rewarding if we strive to enjoy the journey and not just the destination. Viewed like that, any wildlife encounter becomes the icing on the cake. And when an orangutan stares back through soulful eyes, inquisitive penguins waddle past or manta rays circle overhead – the feeling of fulfilment is almost overwhelming.

ENCOUNTERS WITH
TIGERS

"Tiger!' whispers my guide excitedly. Just 30m away, napping in the afternoon sun, lies the **queen of cats**. She stirs; both eyes open and stare, but her gaze is **gentle** and she seems **unfazed** by **our presence**. Even standing this close I feel in no way threatened. Partly keeping an eye on us, she **preens** herself, licking her paws just like a domestic cat. Her chosen spot – a small patch of flattened grass – is a perfect place to hide, her **golden coat** blending into the dry scrub lit by the **fading sun**. Then she stands, stretches and **slinks away**, her black stripes melting into the forest like shadows from the trees."

IAN WOOD

Bengal tigers account for about half of all the tigers surviving in the wild.

THE ENCOUNTER

How and where you choose your encounter with tigers is possibly more important than with any other animal. Get it wrong and you'll be queuing in a long line of packed jeeps just to get a glimpse. But encounter tigers on foot, or on elephant back, or even from a hide, and it will be one of the most powerful wildlife experiences of your life.

Imagine trekking along winding paths up forested hills, punctuated with lakes and open grasslands, knowing that they're out there somewhere. I saw my first tiger after walking for five days and I told myself it didn't matter whether I actually found one. It did, of course: few animals hold such power. Yet they need space to survive and thrive, so finding them requires a combination of patience and expertise. Choose your guide with care and check his/her experience and understanding of these iconic cats.

Of the six subspecies of tiger – Siberian, Indochinese, Malayan, South China, Sumatran and Bengal – the easiest to see is the Bengal tiger, which now accounts for over half of all tigers left in the wild.

A WALK IN THE PARK

Almost anyone who has been on safari will be familiar with the morning and afternoon game drives that become part of your daily routine. You sit back and watch the wildlife from the comfort of the vehicle and it's easy. Yet although jeep safaris can offer some excellent encounters, there is nothing like meeting tigers

▲ Male Bengal tigers are solitary animals with home ranges that can be as large as 75km².

on their own terms. Setting out on foot in tiger country is exhilarating; you're aware that every step could bring you face to face with one of the greatest predators on our planet and that's enough to heighten all your senses. If you are limited by time your chances of meeting a tiger on foot are quite low, but there are places where you can combine shorter walks with jeep safaris. If time is not an issue, then India's Satpura Tiger Reserve has a number of carefully located hides where you wait in long silent vigils; listening to the sounds of the forest; praying for a visit.

ELEPHANT BACK

Sitting astride an elephant brushing through grass and trees in search of tigers; heaven indeed. These silent bulldozers can go anywhere so if you do find a tiger you will have the opportunity of a very close encounter. But be warned, not all elephant treks are what they seem. In some parks in India, 'tiger shows' are set up for mass-market tourism. Once a tiger has been located, hordes of jeeps gather a short distance away while the mahouts arrive with their elephants. Tourists get a very brief ride to see the tiger, which is often surrounded by many other elephants, and the experience can feel extremely commercial. Contrast this with riding for hours through pristine forest with just you and your mahout, and you'll see there's a world of difference.

▲   Elephants are accepted by tigers as being a natural forest animal, allowing passengers to get exceptionally close-up sightings.

TO GO OR NOT TO GO

With an upsurge in the number of people wanting to encounter tigers in the wild, the campaign group Travel Operators for Tigers (TOFT; www.toftigers.org) aims to ensure that tiger tourism develops sustainably. If all those involved, including tour operators, accommodation providers, local services, park management and, of course, visitors, were to join together, it is hoped that would both halt the demise of the tiger and make wildlife tourism in India more responsible. All the tour operators listed here are members of TOFT.

BRIGHT EYES

The tiger's eyes are perfect for night vision but like most cats they can sometimes struggle to see stationary objects. In theory, even a buffalo calf just a few metres away could appear invisible. Not for long though; the mere presence of a prowling cat makes most prey nervous and just the twitch of an ear is enough to catch a tiger's eye. When hunting, tigers also rely on their exceptional hearing, which is so finely tuned that they can tell animals apart by their footfall alone. Their sense of smell on the other hand is not so great and is less useful for finding prey.

ROAR OF APPROVAL

Villagers in India claim that they can hear a tiger roar up to 3km away, which begs the question as to how they know exactly where the tiger is in the first place. What is certain is that their roar can travel quite a distance and is so powerful that it's been known to paralyse some animals on the spot. Humans can only hear noises that have a frequency of between 20 and 20,000 hertz but tigers can produce sounds much lower than this. These low-pitched frequencies, called infrasound, have proved to be the ideal wavelength for travelling long distances; they are even capable of passing through buildings. The theory is still untested, but researchers are confident that this is why some animals have been so rattled by the roar of a tiger that they become literally frozen with fear.

IN BRIEF

SIZE
Male up to 3m/225kg; female up to 2.7m/147kg

STATUS
Bengal, Indochinese, Malayan & Siberian: endangered;
South China & Sumatran: critically endangered.

HOW
Jeep, foot, elephant back & hide

WHO
Foot, hide & elephant 16+
Jeep safari 12+

WHEN
Main season Oct–Apr
Best sightings usually at end of dry season (Feb–Apr)

WHERE
INDIA
• Bandhavgarh National Park
• Corbett National Park
• Kanha Tiger Reserve
• Panna Tiger Reserve
• Pench National Park
• Ranthambore National Park
• Satpura Tiger Reserve

TOURS
www.exodus.co.uk
www.projecttiger.nic.in
www.steppestravel.co.uk
www.wildlifeworldwide.com
www.worldbigcatsafaris.com

FIND OUT MORE
www.globaltigerpatrol.org
www.savethetigerfund.org
www.tigersincrisis.com

 Enjoy the other wildlife if you don't see tigers

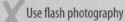 Use flash photography

TRACKING
MOUNTAIN &
LOWLAND GORILLAS

*T*here is no chest beating. In fact, quite the opposite; the silverback can barely stay awake. Occasionally his **deep-set eyes** open to **look at me**, but not for long. I'm flattered that he feels this **relaxed** with me so close. Even in this soporific state his strength **shines** through. Folds of thick black fur, massive hands and nails. When he rouses, he starts to feed, munching on a tender shoot, his **power** reinforced by flashes of his canine teeth. Slightly further back, a baby rolls around on the forest floor, wide-eyed and **innocent**. Mum scoops it up and brings it nearer to her. An **intimate** family scene. "

CHRIS BREEN
www.wildlifeworldwide.com

WILDLIFE WORLDWIDE

THE ENCOUNTER

MOUNTAIN GORILLA Just one hour, that's all you get with mountain gorillas; but I'd go as far to say that it was the greatest hour of my life. Trekking up steep paths, mist hanging in the air; the sense of expectation is enough to make you tingle. Once you're close, there will be a final briefing. In silence you follow your guide, his machete forging a route through the undergrowth. Crouching down in the forest, observing these gentle creatures is a humbling experience. They almost seem out of place, just too big to live here. After 30 minutes, your guide will whisper in your ear; a reminder that you're halfway through. But you'll feel like you've only just arrived.

A certain level of physical fitness is needed to track mountain gorillas and the treks vary according to the location of each group. Walking back from my last encounter in Uganda, we were charged by a silverback. Even our guides were visibly shaken; we retreated and cut another path across the mountain and it took six hours to find our starting point. Exhausted and grazed I joked to my guide, 'So why do people call this the Impenetrable Forest?'

LOWLAND GORILLA The two species of lowland gorilla – western and eastern – have proved much harder to habituate than their mountain cousins. Vegetation at altitude is poor quality, so mountain gorillas have adapted their diet to mainly leaves, stems and roots, which are found everywhere. Quite a contrast

▲   Mountain gorilla tourism is a vital part of conservation, bringing in revenue for both national parks and local communities.
◀◀   Exchanging eye contact with a mountain gorilla offers one of the most profound wildlife experiences anywhere in the world.

to the lush tropical forests, where trees and shrubs are laden with fruit – a lowland gorilla's favourite feast. Their challenge is to find where and when each snack is ripe, forcing them to forage over considerable distances.

Slightly smaller than a mountain gorilla, with shorter brownish fur, lowland gorillas are seen feeding in the trees as well as on the ground. They're more wary of man, too, for they have long been hunted for bush meat. Add in the reduced visibility in these dense forests and you'll see why quality encounters – compared with mountain gorillas – are much rarer.

NUMBERS GAME

Mountain gorilla tourism is a conservation success story, yet with only 786 mountain gorillas in 2010, there might seem to be little cause for optimism. The good news is that 480 of these live in Africa's Virunga Massif, an area encompassing national parks in Rwanda, Uganda and the Democratic Republic of Congo (DRC). The population here has been closely watched for over half a century and these latest figures show an increase of over 26% in just seven years. Today there are more gorillas thriving here than in the early sixties, and nearly twice as many as in 1981.

Permits to see the gorillas are expensive but this income is used both to protect their habitat and to help local communities. Add in the other money that you'll spend during your trip and you'll see why ecotourism is now the most important industry in both Rwanda and Uganda. Hopefully, with more stability in the DRC, the same will apply there in future years. If current projects to habituate more lowland gorillas prove successful then this should in turn help to protect these animals and open up tourism in new areas.

ADDED BONUS

Bamboo forests in Uganda and Rwanda have other primates lurking in their shadows. Golden monkeys are notoriously shy and it's taken years of patient work to get them used to people. You creep around as they move almost silently through the trees – it's a cat-and-mouse affair. But catch them in a ray of sunlight and you'll see their luminescent faces, peeking through the foliage, gentle eyes staring back at you.

▲ Two groups of golden monkeys have been habituated: one in Rwanda's Volcanoes National Park, and the other in Mgahinga National Park, Uganda.

▸▸ Lowland gorillas typically forage over greater distances than mountain gorillas.

GENTLE GIANT

Gorillas may have immense strength but they are shy and gentle creatures, with man their only real enemy. The undisputed leader of each group of mountain gorillas, the silverback, has quite a responsibility. He decides where his group will forage, rest and sleep, along with arbitrating any family disputes. But if his unit is threatened, either by humans or a rival group, he'll use his mighty power to protect them, even at the cost of his own life.

SIGN OF THE TIMES

Koko is a western lowland gorilla who has lived at the San Francisco Zoo since her birth in 1971. When, a year later, Dr Francine 'Penny' Patterson started a four-year postgraduate project with Koko, she started teaching her American sign language. Koko showed such a natural ability that teaching her has become Penny's life's work – with quite remarkable results. At first, Penny taught the gorilla some basic signs and monitored her responses, but then Koko began to make up her own. Often these would combine two words that she'd learnt; for example, 'eye hat' was used to express the word 'mask'. Today she has a vocabulary of over 1,000 signs and can understand more than 2,000 words of spoken English. Quite impressive when you consider that the average human uses fewer in everyday speech.

IN BRIEF

SIZE
Mountain gorilla
Male to 1.8m/220kg; female to 1.2m/135kg

Western lowland gorilla
Male to 1.7m/180kg; female to 1.2m/90kg

Eastern lowland gorilla
Male to 1.8m/210kg; female to 1.2m/100kg

STATUS
Mountain gorilla & eastern lowland, endangered;
western lowland, critically endangered

HOW
Trekking

WHO
15+

WHEN
• Rwanda, Uganda, DRC: all year; short wet seasons
  Mar–Apr, Oct–Nov
• Central African Republic: Nov–Apr
• Gabon: Oct–Mar
• Cameroon: Dec–Aug
• Republic of the Congo: Jun–Aug

WHERE
Mountain gorilla
1 DRC
• Virunga National Park

2 RWANDA
• Volcanoes National Park

3 UGANDA
• Bwindi Impenetrable & Mgahinga Gorilla
  National Parks

Western lowland gorilla
4 CAMEROON
• Deng Deng National Park

5 CENTRAL AFRICAN REPUBLIC
• Dzanga-Ndoki National Park

6 GABON
• Lopé National Park

7 REPUBLIC OF THE CONGO
• Odzala National Park

Eastern lowland gorilla
8 DRC
• Kahuzi-Biega National Park

TOURS
www.wildlifeworldwide.com (see page 178)
www.agoodplace.co.uk
www.steppesdiscovery.co.uk
www.worldprimatesafaris.com

FIND OUT MORE
www.gorillafund.org
www.gorillas.org
www.igcp.org

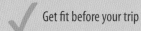 Get fit before your trip

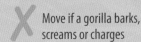 Move if a gorilla barks,
screams or charges

TRACKING
CHIMPANZEES

"*We're on the move, brushing through the trees in dense forest. In the distance I can already hear a **chorus of shrieks** and calls. It's **exciting** tracking a troop of chimpanzees; this is no static encounter. As we stop to catch our breath, there's a huge **commotion** quite close by – screeching and banging on tree trunks, but no sightings – yet. We set off again, faster, scrambling towards the noise. There's a movement in the trees but I catch no more than **a glimpse** of our closest relative. Then, in a moment of calm – almost silence – I spot him. A large male chimpanzee stares back, **inquisitive**. His scrutiny lasts just a few seconds, then he's off again, crashing through the trees with the rest of the troop as we follow in pursuit.*"

IAN WOOD

THE ENCOUNTER

Dawn is the best time to track chimpanzees in the wild. The air smells fresh and clean; birds are singing and there's a feeling of peace and tranquillity – until you hear them. Grunts, squeals, bangs, hoots; so much of this experience is about the noises that they make.

You can't always remain on paths while tracking chimpanzees – sometimes you'll be roaming through virgin jungle. It's advisable to wear long-sleeved shirts and trousers to avoid insect bites, along with comfortable walking boots or trainers. Groups are led by knowledgeable guides who know these forests well. While viewing is limited to an hour, your total time in the forest will be slightly longer – depending on how long it has taken to locate the troop. First sightings are often a blur but you'll creep closer, always keeping at least ten metres away. Sometimes, an expressive face peeks backs through the vegetation, but don't count on the chimps staying still for long. They usually don't!

RULES OF ENGAGEMENT

Chimpanzees are our closest living relatives, sharing over 98% of the same DNA, so they are extremely prone to human diseases. It is essential that you do not track chimpanzees if you have any infectious disease or feel unwell. Visitors should be restricted to a maximum number of six per group and viewing time limited to one hour to minimise the disturbance to both the chimpanzees and the forest.

▲ The chimpanzees in Gombe Stream National Park are the subject of the world's longest-running study of any wild animal.
◄◄ Chimpanzees have a varied diet including fruits, leaves, nuts, mushrooms, insects and meat.

CHIMPANZEE ORPHANAGES

It's extremely hard to release captured chimpanzees back into the wild as they are likely to be rejected, injured or killed by existing populations. For the lucky few – rescued from zoos, circuses and the pet trade – a new life begins in an orphanage where the chimps reign supreme. Although these don't offer a wild encounter, many do afford close-up meetings with their primate guests, especially at feeding time; and at Uganda's Ngamba Chimpanzee Sanctuary, nestled on an island in Lake Victoria, you can walk through the forest or even arrange to be a personal chimp carer for the day.

SIZE MATTERS

When it comes to the size of testicles, chimpanzees win compared with gorillas and humans; in fact their unfeasibly large gonads are in a different league. Despite being the largest primate, gorilla bits weigh in at about 28 grammes per pair, with humans averaging over 40 grammes. Contrast these figures with the whopping 110 grammes for chimpanzees and you'll see why we've long puzzled over this mystery. And it all comes down to insecurities. As a general rule, the more promiscuous the females are within a species, the larger the testicles of the males. So male gorillas get away with it as they live in closed societies where they keep an eye on their women. But female chimps mate with several partners and, faced with such stiff competition, males produce more sperm and hence boast larger testes.

MOB RULE

Chimpanzees share their forests with several other primates, including red colobus monkeys. Occasionally, you'll spot their small faces through the dense leaves, their fur decorated with shades of orange, white and black. But chimpanzees aren't impressed by their appearance. Acting in a gang, they sometimes brutally hunt them down, isolating the infants and juveniles, which are then beaten to death. Chimpanzees don't eat meat very often, but when they catch these monkeys they consume almost everything, including the brain.

▲   Red colobus monkeys use their colour vision to select the youngest leaves, which are higher in proteins and easier to digest.
▶▶ Chimpanzees form close family bonds that can last a lifetime.

FAMILY LIFE

Like us, chimpanzees are emotional animals. They form close bonds that last a lifetime and mothers nurture their offspring with intimate love for the first decade of their lives. Siblings and other females lend a hand with child care and if a mother is injured or killed, these other members of the troop will take over her duties. Studies have shown that abused chimpanzees show all the symptoms of post-traumatic stress disorder: a strong argument for banning their use in British laboratory experiments in 1998.

Yet being so closely related to humans means that chimpanzees also have a darker side. In Tanzania's Gombe Stream National Park, Jane Goodall has documented a number of violent interactions, perhaps the most shocking of which was when a dominant male known as Figan took his troop to war against a sub-community. His strategy was brutal: hunt them down, attack them using teeth, hands and feet, and leave them to die. Over four years they killed all the males and at least one female of the other troop – chilling when you consider that these chimpanzees were previously both companions and grooming partners.

IN BRIEF

SIZE
Male up to 1.2m/70kg
Female up to 1m/50kg

STATUS
Endangered

HOW
Trekking

WHO
16+

WHEN & WHERE
1 KENYA
• Sweetwaters Game Reserve (all year)

2 RWANDA
• Nyungwe Forest (all year; wettest months Apr–May & Oct–Nov)

3 TANZANIA
All year; dry seasons May–Oct & Jan–Feb
• Mahale Mountains National Park
• Gombe Stream National Park

4 UGANDA
All year; wettest months Apr–May & Oct–Nov
• Kibale Forest National Park
• Budongo Forest Reserve
• Kyambura Gorge
• Ngamba Island (www.ngambaisland.com)

5 ZAMBIA Chimfunshi Wildlife Orphanage (all year)
www.chimfunshi.org.za

TOURS
www.expertafrica.com
www.steppesdiscovery.co.uk
www.wildlifeworldwide.com
www.worldprimatesafaris.com

FIND OUT MORE
www.chimpworlds.com
www.janegoodall.org

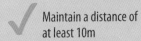 Maintain a distance of at least 10m

 Eat or drink while you are near chimpanzees

UP CLOSE WITH
ORANGUTANS

> The forest **hums** with the **chatter** of insects and birds. Sweat trickles down my neck and dissolves into my already soaking shirt. This is Borneo, **land of the orangutan**. We hear him first: a **crack of wood** like a single gunshot. As he stretches out an enormous arm to grab the next branch, I get my first good look at him. Then he stops; he's noticed us. **Shafts of sunlight** spark his orange fur as he stares down upon his silent audience. His deep eyes, framed on either side by colossal cheek pads, draw me in. I see **power**, **peace** and **wisdom**. I wonder what he sees in me.

IAN WOOD

◀ Baby orangutans are dependent on their mothers for up to eight years — longer than any other primate apart from humans.

THE ENCOUNTER

There are two different species of orangutan: one confined to the island of Borneo; the other to Sumatra. There are certainly more orangutans in Borneo, currently about 45,000, compared with fewer than 7,000 in Sumatra, but both offer opportunities for excellent encounters with these great apes.

Wild orangutans are usually very shy of people and most of the time you'll only see them high in trees. Your best chance of meeting them up close is to visit a rehabilitation centre where orphaned orangutans have been released back into the jungle. These usually have some kind of feeding platform in the forest where fruit is placed at certain times of day. Here, the orangutans have become very used to people and it's not unusual for them to come extremely close. Looking into their eyes, you'll feel a powerful connection – but always remember that they can be unpredictable.

Orangutans' teeth are razor sharp, so never try to initiate any contact and always give them space; as a general rule try to stay at least five metres away. And if a male orangutan charges at you – run. Standing your ground – although recommended with gorillas – is simply not an option.

THE BATTLE FOR SURVIVAL

Tourism is one element in the battle to protect orangutan habitat and ensure that these great apes have a future in the wild. Visitors send out a positive message to both local and international governments

▲   Tanjung Puting National Park in Borneo offers extraordinary close encounters with these great apes.
▶   Orangutans can often be observed using leaves like an umbrella to keep them dry in tropical downpours.
▶▶   Using pursed lips, orangutans make a kiss-squeak call if they feel threatened.

  FOREST

and also provide jobs for guides, hotel staff, etc. If you use a tour company, ask them if they make a contribution from your trip towards orangutan conservation.

COLOUR CLASH

Orangutans are famous for their reddish orange fur, which looks spectacular illuminated by the sun, but in the depths of the forest they blend in seamlessly with the trees. This is caused by the jungle vegetation, which absorbs the red and orange spectrum of sunlight, leaving orangutans looking a lot duller than you'd imagine – and much harder to spot in their natural environment.

SEX LIFE

You need to like your own company if you're a male orangutan. For most primates, including human beings, contact with other members of their species is pretty important, yet these great apes will do almost anything to avoid it. If this prompts the question as to how they find a mate, the answer is as old as the hills: when a male orangutan wants sex he can suddenly turn on the charm. From nowhere he finds a set of social skills that makes him look positively smooth. He follows her through the forest for days on end, making luxurious nests each evening. The new lovers mate frequently and he'll even share his precious fruit. But nothing lasts forever, so love what you have while you have it. Within just two weeks, she'll have rejected him and he'll return to his life of solitude.

A GIANT LEAP

Many other primates share the forest with orangutans, but gibbons are the true masters of jungle locomotion. Swinging from branch to branch they can move at bewildering speed, covering distances of over ten metres in one go. But you are far more likely to hear these agile primates than see them, as their melodious songs break the morning stillness of the forest. Made by an adult pair – which mate for life – these calls help to claim their territory and warn intruders to stay away.

CALL OF THE WILD

The long call of a sexually mature male orangutan – an unmistakable series of booming pulses and grumbles – can travel for over a kilometre through dense forest. Used to attract females, it also serves to warn other males to stay away from his territory. Orangutans also make a 'kiss squeak' call by taking a sharp intake of air through pursed lips. If you're walking through the jungle and you come across an orangutan who isn't habituated to humans, you'll sometimes hear this warning cry – an announcement that it feels threatened by your presence.

IN BRIEF

SIZE
Male to 1.6m/60–90kg
Female to 1.2m/30–45kg

STATUS
Borneo orangutan: endangered
Sumatran orangutan: critically endangered

HOW
Trekking & river boat

WHO
10+

WHEN
All year; dry season Apr–Oct

WHERE
1 INDONESIA
• Bohorok Rehabilitation Centre, Bukit Lawang, Sumatra
• Ketambe, Gunung Leseur National Park, Sumatra
• Tanjung Puting National Park, Borneo

2 MALAYSIA
• Danum Valley Wildlife Reserve, Borneo
• Sepilok Orangutan Sanctuary

TOURS
www.agoodplace.co.uk
www.steppestravel.co.uk
www.wildlifeworldwide.com
www.worldprimatesafaris.com

FIND OUT MORE
www.orangutan.org.uk
www.savetheorangutan.co.uk
www.sumatranorangutan.org

 Remain silent in their presence

 Initiate any contact

PRIMATE COMMUNICATIONS

Encounters with primates are rarely silent affairs. Haunting songs of gibbons echoing through the forest; macaques screeching in the trees; growls, grunts and whoops as chimpanzees forage in the jungle. Living in social groups, primates also use body language – teeth bared, forehead raised, staring eyes – and in many close-up sightings you'll have some aimed at you.

With spiked blond hair and heart-shaped patterns on their chests, gelada baboons have a look that many a transvestite would be proud of. Clear communications are essential for these grass-eating primates which sometimes gather in their hundreds. A shrill bark is used to warn of imminent danger and will send the whole group fleeing for cover. Rhythmic grunts signal friendly intentions and males will boom a deep low repeating bark to reinforce their status. Their most noticeable facial expression is reserved to show displeasure. Staring, they raise their eyebrows to show more whites of their eyes and then grimace with an open-mouthed yawn.

TOURS www.steppestravel.co.uk
WHERE & WHEN Ethiopia Simien Mountains (all year)

▶ Gelada baboons are nicknamed 'bleeding-heart baboons' due to the red heart-shaped patterns on their chests.

Direct eye contact and staring is a threat display shared by many different primates. Get too close to macaques and they'll gaze back at you, retracting their scalps and showing rows of teeth. Some troops of **Japanese macaques** – or more commonly snow monkeys – have taken to bathing in hot springs. It's soporific, watching them relaxing in the water, preening one another, hot steam rising in the air. But look them in the eyes and these placid primates will soon turn aggressive, snarling with teeth bared – a warning to back off.

TOURS www.insidejapantours.com

WHERE & WHEN Japan Jigokudani Monkey Park (Dec–Mar)

Casual sex is the way that **bonobos** do it, lubricating – quite literally – their gears of social harmony. Observing these primates is not for the prudish. Sex is used for nearly any purpose from bonding and making up after disputes to easing tensions in the troop. Like humans', the female bonobo's genitals are positioned slightly forward, allowing face-to-face intercourse. Not that they restrict themselves to this. Gay sex, group sex, cunnilingus, fellatio and sex with food are all used as forms of communication – as casually as we might use a subtle smile or a handshake.

TOURS www.worldprimatesafaris.com

WHERE & WHEN Democratic Republic of Congo Salonga National Park (all year)

Golden snub-nosed monkeys are the ventriloquists of the primate world, able to vocalise a range of sounds without moving their lips or face. Living in large groups helps to fend off predators and they've developed 18 different calls. Five of these are reserved for alarm signals, ranging from a light early-warning call to frightened shrieks of panic. An individual troop consists of one male and several females but they'll band together with other groups to roam the forest in larger numbers. Contacting calls are reserved for greeting other troops, to signify peaceful intentions.

TOURS www.wildchina.com

WHERE & WHEN China Xi'an-Foping Natural Reserve (Nov–Mar)

Japanese macaques live in large troops that can number several hundred individuals.

Together with chimpanzees, bonobos are our closest living relative.

Native to central China, golden snub-nosed monkeys spend almost their entire lives in trees.

INQUISITIVE
LEMURS

"*Hands held high – like **awkward ballerinas** – a troop of sifaka lemurs **dances** across the forest clearing. Oblivious to my presence, they bounce sideways in a two-legged hopping style, long tails swinging out behind. **Sunlight flickers** through the trees, **illuminating** their white fur with an extra sheen – and adding contrast to their dark faces and feet. But when they spot me, their dance routine comes to an abrupt halt. With an extra spring in their step they **leap effortlessly** up to the lower branches of a tree. From their new vantage point, it's **them watching me** now: staring down through bright **mischievous** eyes surrounded by black blobs.*"

IAN WOOD

◀ Sifaka lemurs use their powerful hind legs to jump from tree to tree and are capable of clearing distances of up to nine metres.

THE ENCOUNTER

Lemurs are easy to see in several parts of Madagascar, but are found nowhere else in the world apart from the neighbouring Comoros Islands. New species are still being identified, but the most instantly recognisable are the ring-tailed and the sifaka – the latter famous for its sideways dancing.

In some places, lemurs are so accustomed to humans that they have almost become pests. Take the Berenty Reserve, for example. The trails are wide and the lemurs friendly and abundant. Sitting having breakfast in the early morning sun, I was joined by a mother and baby lemur in the chair opposite. This is the result of lemurs being fed by humans for years and it isn't natural behaviour. Not that I'm knocking it – in fact I loved having lemurs for company – but the waiter aggressively chased them off.

Contrast this with trekking through dry forests to meet lemurs in the wild; listening to their barks and screeches as you follow through the trees; or waiting in a forest clearing – hoping that they'll dance across.

Never get too close to lemurs: they can bite. And keep an eye on your possessions. Leave a bag unattended, and you could well find the contents scattered across the ground.

ODOUR DE LEMUR

Sense of smell is vital for a lemur as this is one of their main forms of communication. With scent glands on the bottoms of their feet, they leave their signature on every surface to mark their territories. But during the mating season, the male ring-tailed lemur goes one step further, covering his tail with smelly secretions and waving it in the air. What female could refuse such charm?

▲ Conspicuous with their tails held aloft, ring-tailed lemurs are the most terrestrial of all the lemur species, spending considerable time on the forest floor.

BEAUTY IS SKIN DEEP

Chameleons are the quick-change artists of the reptile world, and scores of different species live in Madagascan forests. Catch them at the right moment and you can watch their vivid colours and patterns morph before your eyes: browns to yellows; reds to greens and blues. Sitting on a branch, they'll roll their bulging eyes — as if they're thinking — before a tongue flies out to snatch an insect meal.

SHRINKING FORESTS

Slash-and-burn agriculture, mining and illegal logging have contributed to the loss of about 90% of Madagascar's forests, with severe effects on its lemur population. Yet at last there are signs for cautious optimism. Ranomafana National Park is now listed as a UNESCO World Heritage Site with over 100,000 acres of protected land. Half the revenue generated from entrance fees is distributed to villagers living on its borders, providing direct incentives to conserve this region.

IN BRIEF

SIZE
From pygmy mouse lemur, 12cm/30g, to indri, 72cm/7kg

STATUS
Ten species critically endangered; seven endangered; 19 vulnerable

HOW
On foot

WHO
No age limit

WHEN
Dry season (Apr–Nov)

WHERE
MADAGASCAR
- Andasibe-Mantadia National Park ('Perinet')
- Ankarafantsika National Park ('Ampijoroa')
- Ankarana Special Reserve
- Berenty Private Reserve & Ifotaka Community Forest
- Isalo National Park & Zombitse Forest National Park
- Kirindy Forest
- Marojejy National Park
- Nosy Mangabe Island Reserve & Masoala National Park
- Ranomafana National Park

TOURS
www.rainbowtours.co.uk
www.wildlifeworldwide.com
www.worldprimatesafaris.com

FIND OUT MORE
www.savethelemur.org
www.wildmadagascar.org

 Keep an eye on your possessions

 Feed lemurs

PROBOSCIS MONKEYS
FROM THE RIVER

“*I*t's late afternoon. Framed on either side by **verdant jungle**, we're chugging along a river in Borneo. Above the drone of our engine, there's a honking noise, rising and falling like a broken siren, drawing our eyes to a shape high up in the tree. **Silhouetted** by the **fading sun**, his massive nose and pot belly look comical as he rocks the branch back and forth. Then, arms outstretched, he hurls himself – a **giant leap of faith**. The crash-landing in the other tree is far from graceful, but one by one his family follow. Climbing high, they settle on the branches – the male positioned slightly lower, **keeping guard**. Silence now; his harem is safely perched around him, long tails hanging down. As **dusk descends**, their orange colour fades; greyish shadows merging with the trees.*

IAN WOOD”

◀ Using their long tails to help them balance, proboscis monkeys sleep high in the trees along the river banks.

THE ENCOUNTER

Proboscis monkeys live only in Borneo, confined to low-lying coastal forest swamps. Every evening, small groups gather in treetops next to a river, so heading out by boat offers the best chance to get close. Although dusk is good, some of my favourite encounters have been in the very early morning, when the mist clings to the surface of the water. As the sun rises, the monkeys start their day, often moving through the trees in a 'follow my leader' routine; if one jumps, the rest will usually follow. Occasionally, they will even cross rivers: hurling themselves from branches and crashing into the water, then frantically swimming doggy-paddle style to the other side, hoping to avoid the crocodiles lurking in the swamp. But despite these antics, they are quite shy of humans, so approaching slowly and quietly is key.

MONKEY BUSINESS

Savage deforestation over the last two decades has had a devastating impact on Borneo's low-lying swamps, yet tourism sends out positive signals to the Malaysian and Indonesian governments that Borneo's wildlife is valuable. Despite the gloom, one of the most important

GLOW IN THE DARK

Paddling along a river in Borneo after dusk, you may be joined by fireflies, twinkling like Christmas tree lights on palms at the water's edge. Congregating in large numbers, they flash signals back and forth as a means of communication — but it also serves another purpose. Their abdomens are filled with a nasty-tasting chemical which emits the light, so once a potential predator gets a taste, they learn to leave these bugs alone.

Proboscis monkeys are famous for their spectacular leaps, sometimes hurtling themselves in the air before crash-landing in another tree
With enormous pendulous noses, male proboscis monkeys are almost twice the size of the females.

populations of proboscis monkeys thrives in Tanjung Puting National Park, where you'll see so many that it's easy to forget how endangered these primates are.

OVERSIZED

Male proboscis monkeys are well endowed in the nasal department, with bigger noses than any other primate. Reaching up to 17cm long, their impressive conks are so large that sometimes you'll see the monkeys pushing them out of their way to eat. It seems that a large nose is quite an asset in terms of attracting females, but it's not all about vanity. When proboscis monkeys are threatened, their noses swell even more and act as a kind of resonating chamber to amplify their warning call.

Talking of supersized endowments, consider those pot bellies. No, these aren't a result of overeating; rather, the monkey's stomachs are distended by the number of digestive departments needed to break down their diet of leaves. This process is extremely slow and their stomachs can contain up to a quarter of an individual's body weight.

IN BRIEF

SIZE
Male up to 78cm/21kg;
female up to 65cm/10kg

STATUS
Endangered

HOW
Riverboat

WHO
No age restriction

WHEN
All year; dry season Apr–Oct

WHERE
1 BRUNEI
• Brunei River, near Bandar Seri Begawan

2 INDONESIA
• Tanjung Puting National Park, Borneo

3 MALAYSIA
• Baku National Park
• Danum Valley Wildlife Reserve
• River Sanctuary
• Labuk Bay Proboscis Monkey Sanctuary

TOURS
www.agoodplace.co.uk
www.steppestravel.co.uk
www.wildlifeworldwide.com

FIND OUT MORE
www.proboscismonkey.org
www.proboscis.cc

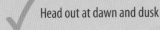 Head out at dawn and dusk

 Make any noise or sudden movements as you approach

WALKING IN THE
COSTA RICAN
RAINFOREST

'We are declaring peace with nature,' said Mario Fernández Silva, the ambassador of Costa Rica. 'Until we know what we have, it is our duty to protect it.' The world is bored of politicians making false promises, but Costa Rica has delivered by abolishing its army and using funds from taxes to conserve its biodiversity. The result? Forest cover has risen from 24% in 1985 to over 45% today.

▲ About a quarter of Costa Rica's landmass is now protected by national parks and reserves.

FOREST

Walking in the Monteverde cloudforest of Costa Rica is like stepping into the Lost World. Dangling roots and vines sweep across the trails and the entire forest is decorated with pearls of moisture, dripping from every leaf, fern and flower. Above the cacophony of humming insects and the constant chirping of birds, listen for another sound – the deep guttural growl of the howler monkey. Early morning is best, when small troops roam through the treetops in search of fruit and leaves.

Often you'll spot wildlife by such noises, or by looking for movements in the trees, but not so with the sloth. These legendary slow movers look like primates, but they are more closely related to armadillos and anteaters. Both the two-toed and three-toed varieties make their homes high up in Costa Rican forests, with the latter more active during the day – and thus more visible.

Adding contrast to the forest palette are Costa Rica's birds, with nearly 900 species recorded. With bills designed to feed on different flowers, tiny hummingbirds hover on wings that move at over 100 beats a second. That's too fast for the human eye to follow, but find them sucking nectar and you'll be able to see their vibrant colours quite close up. The sound of two melancholic notes – one rising, the other falling – is the call of the quetzal. Like most birds, the male is more glamorous, with crimson breast and two long green-and-white tail feathers which can trail over a metre.

With so much life in the trees, it's easy to forget to look down, but here too wildlife abounds. Keep your eyes peeled for long trails of leaf-cutter ants, which can carry leaves much larger than their bodies. A colony can run into several million and can move over 20 tonnes of soil to build their nests.

Frogs and toads inhabit the forest floor, too. Among them, you can't miss the garish colours of the poison-dart frogs. Their moist skin – laden with toxins – enhances their colours with a glossy sheen, warning potential predators to stay away. Rarely dangerous to humans, the toxin is used by some tribes to tip arrows as an aid to killing prey.

One of the things that makes Costa Rica so special is the sheer variety of species that live within its limited borders. While it has only 0.25% of the world's landmass, it contains about 5% of the world's biodiversity. No wonder then, that ecotourism is its most important source of income.

▲ LEFT In breeding season, male quetzals grow tail feathers that can trail up to a metre long.
▲ CENTRE Howler monkeys have large throats and shell-like vocal chambers to amplify their calls.
▲ RIGHT Sloths are capable of sleeping up to 20 hours in a single day.

WATCHING
GRIZZLY BEARS
CATCH SALMON

"*Splashing along, he constantly* **scans the water** *– no time for a second glance at me, not with salmon on his mind. He stops briefly – eyes ever alert – then* **rears up** *and* **pounces***; huge paddy paws jab into the river. Water sprays around him and there's his prize – a gleaming fish. Further upstream, another bear has a* **far more elegant** *approach. Standing on some rocks by a series of small rapids he simply waits. Every now and then his favourite food jumps out of the water and he neatly* **catches it mid-air***. But prime position is reserved for the largest bear, who brooks* **no rivals***. Sitting in a pool at the base of the falls, he's lazily grabbing his lunch as it passes on the watery conveyor-belt – or* **feasting on salmon** *that fail in their leap.*"

IAN WOOD

THE ENCOUNTER

A grizzly bear needs to eat a lot of food to put on enough fat to see it through the winter. So when salmon spawn, you can usually be sure of finding bears. It's a narrow window of opportunity for you and the bears – somewhere in the region of just six weeks – but time it right and you will be rewarded with one of nature's great encounters.

In some places, such as Brooks Falls in Alaska, there are raised platforms overlooking the river where you can safely watch bears roaming just a few metres away – perhaps even beneath your vantage point. Elsewhere, how close you will be able to get is ultimately down to the bears themselves. When you first find grizzlies, your guide will evaluate a safe and respectful distance to watch them from. This depends on several things such as the movement and activity of the bears, whether you're watching from a boat or from land, and the number and behaviour of other people at the site. Individual bears can sometimes total a dozen or so on the same stretch of river and, once your position is established, may well approach to within under ten metres.

▲ In places such as Brook Falls, Alaska, viewing platforms allow extremely close but safe encounters with grizzly bears.
◀◀ Feasting on salmon helps grizzly bears gain sufficient weight to see them through the winter months.

  FOREST

ADDED BONUS

Bald eagles are near-certain attendants where grizzly bears are catching salmon — swooping down to finish off the fish that the bears leave behind. Despite their size — most have a wingspan of over two metres — they're much more timid than they look; occasionally they'll even be shooed away from fish carcasses by much smaller birds. There is always the chance to spot a black bear too, but you will need a generous slice of luck to glimpse the shy and elusive wolves that prowl these forests.

THE BEAR ESSENTIALS

Grizzly-bear viewing is extremely popular, so consideration needs to be given to where and how you undertake this encounter. The mere presence of humans near to bears can create stress and even cause them to abandon their habitat – temporarily or permanently. Viewers can also be at risk if bears become too familiar and lose their natural shyness of people. It is therefore essential to choose trips that are run by experts in both bears and conservation.

IN BRIEF

SIZE
Up to 1.5–3m upright/200–350kg

STATUS
Threatened

HOW
Boat, platform & foot

WHO
10 +

WHEN & WHERE
1 CANADA
• Bella Coola River, Tweedsmuir Provincial Park, British Columbia (Aug–Sep)
• Knight Inlet, British Columbia (Jul–Sep)
• Fishing Branch River, Ni'iinlii Njik Territorial Park, Yukon (Jun–Sep)

2 USA
• Brooks Falls, Katmai National Park, Alaska (Jul & Sep)
• McNeil River Sanctuary, Alaska (Jul–Aug)
• Wolverine Creek, Lake Clark National Park, Alaska (Jun–Aug)

TOURS
www.greatbeartours.com
www.steppestravel.co.uk
www.wildlifeworldwide.com
www.worldbearsafaris.com

FIND OUT MORE
www.bearsmart.com
www.bearviewing.ca
www.greatbear.org

 Stay together in a tight group

 Consume any food while watching bears

EURASIAN BROWN BEARS
FROM A HIDE

"The warm summer evening makes it feel sticky in the hide. Three of us, peering out, wait in silence. On every breath, my nostrils taste the outside air – pine **fresh from the forest**. Just so many insects; clouds of midges everywhere. Two hours later and I'm feeling soporific – until a **sound of snapping wood** jolts me wide awake. There, **emerging** from the trees, is a bear. Its **golden fur** is frizzled at the edges by the fading sun. Lolloping in our direction, it stops close to the hide before **drawing itself up** to its full eight-foot height. Ears alerted by the sounds of clicking cameras, it **looks straight towards us**, eyes trying to focus – like an old man squinting."

IAN WOOD

THE ENCOUNTER

Along the border of Finland and Russia lies an area of untouched wilderness. Frozen in an icy winter for eight months each year, the taiga forests are home to several hundred brown bears. Not that you're likely to see them on foot – these lumbering giants have a natural fear of man following years of persecution. But there is another way: become nocturnal and head for a hide.

For some 20 years, brown bears have been lured to feeding stations where bait is left. Overlooking these areas are a number of strategically positioned hides, providing the perfect vantage point to spy on the bears. Although it's essential that you don't make any noise, the bears have become accustomed to the sound of cameras, allowing you to photograph them at extremely close quarters. There will be long periods of inactivity, until suddenly the sounds of twigs snapping and leaves rustling will signal that you have company. It's not uncommon to see a fully grown adult just metres away, or to observe a female with a group of playful cubs.

In peak summer (May–July), daylight lingers here for over 20 hours. You arrive late afternoon and spend the whole night waiting in silence. But these hides aren't just rustic shacks; comfortable chairs are provided for up to ten people and some even have bunk beds so you can sleep during the hours of darkness. In the morning you retreat to your accommodation, half-an-hour's walk away, to rest and regroup – ready for the next evening's mission.

▲   Fiercely protective, a mother Eurasian brown bear cares for her cubs for up to three years before they are ready to face life on their own.
▶   When standing upright, brown bears can tower up to three metres.
◀◀   Truly omnivorous, brown bears are opportunistic hunters with a diverse diet including rabbits, fish, rodents, insects, roots, berries and nuts.

SKUNK BEAR

Other visitors are possible while you are lurking in your hide. With shaggy brown fur, wolverines look like miniature bears that have grown long bushy tails. About the size of a medium dog, they are members of the weasel family and you will probably smell them first — an unpleasant pungent aroma that gives rise to their nickname, 'skunk bear'. Long stretches of time also affords fantastic opportunities for birdwatching, with ravens, hawks, owls, eagles and woodpeckers often seen.

BACK FROM THE BRINK

Eurasian brown bears are still at risk from habitat destruction, forcing them to roam in smaller areas. This can lead to unwanted human–bear contact which is used as a justification for governments handing out hunting licences. But parts of Scandinavia have seen an increase in bear numbers in recent years due to conservation efforts. Responsibly organised bear tours provide a way of supporting such projects while enabling people to enjoy these creatures in their natural setting.

IN BRIEF

SIZE
Up to 3m upright/350kg

STATUS
Least concern

HOW
Hide

WHO
16+

WHEN
Apr–Sep

WHERE
1 FINLAND
• Kuhmo
• Martinselkonen Nature Reserve

2 ROMANIA
• Carpathian Mountains

3 SWEDEN
• Hälsingland Forest

TOURS
www.wbb.fi
www.martinselkonen.fi
www.wildlifeworldwide.com
www.wildsweden.com

FIND OUT MORE
www.bb.fi
www.bearproject.info

 Remember insect repellent

 Make any noise

TREKKING IN SEARCH OF
KOMODO DRAGONS

"The scorching sun has reduced most of the foliage to brown dry scrub. I **catch the waft** of an odd aroma: not a pleasant one – somewhere between rotting meat and bad breath. Then a **sudden rustle** in the grass startles us and our guide jumps backwards, wielding his stick in front of him. '**Move, move!**' he shouts, with such **urgency** that it causes panic. Safely further down the track, we regroup and watch the dragon from a distance. Still heading towards us, it **plods** on short stubby feet – while its **forked tongue slithers** in and out. We're ready to retreat again, but about seven metres short, it stops and stares at us through cold **menacing eyes**. An uneasy stand-off – until eventually it turns and **skulks** away."

IAN WOOD

THE ENCOUNTER

Trekking in search of Komodo dragons will lead you up gentle paths, affording views over the surrounding islands. Aquamarine water shimmers in the sunlight, dotted with green blobs of land rising from the ocean. Yet coming face to face with giant lizards is a chilling experience. They have little or no fear of humans and have even been known to kill. Using their strong powerful legs, they are capable of short bursts of speed, so when instructed you need to move promptly.

Most treks take two guides – armed with thick wooden staffs – to ward away a dragon if it tries to get too close. Fortunately their eyesight isn't great, but they make up for this with an acute sense of smell, detecting potential prey and blood from several kilometres away. As such, if you have an open wound or are menstruating you won't be allowed to join a trek. Komodo dragons are highly territorial, often spotted lurking near paths, where deer and other prey roam. But keep an eye up high as well: younger dragons avoid fights by climbing trees.

DRAGON CONSERVATION

The Komodo dragon is a vulnerable species whose numbers are dwindling because of habitat loss. Despite that, they represent a serious risk for local communities; recently an eight-year-old boy was killed while playing in long grass near his home. But the lure of trekking brings in badly needed revenue for this remote

▲ Considered a myth until 1912, Komodo dragons are one of the most fearsome reptiles on our planet.
◥ Sulphur-crested cockatoos live in the wild for up to 40 years, which is about half as long as in captivity.
◀◀ Komodo dragons are the world's largest reptile, reaching lengths of up to three metres.

  FOREST

region, creating jobs for guides, homestay hosts and boat crews, who in turn help to defend the lizard's habitat.

FOUL MOUTHED

The saliva of a Komodo dragon contains at least four types of toxic bacteria and its teeth can harbour bits of rotting meat from past meals. Blood from their gums adds to this appealing blend, making their breath quite foul and their mouths deadly. A Komodo dragon's bite causes wounds that are extremely slow to heal and then become infected. Although not always successful in bringing down a larger animal, the dragon will track its weakened prey until it dies. The puzzle is how they can sustain such virulent bacteria in their mouths, but not be at risk of it themselves. Scientists think that the answer may lie in their immune systems and are now studying Komodo dragons to see if they can isolate what appears to be an antibacterial molecule.

IN BRIEF

SIZE
Up to 3m/80kg

STATUS
Vulnerable

HOW
Trekking

WHO
16+

WHEN
All year; dry season Apr–Nov

WHERE
INDONESIA
• Komodo
• Padar
• Rinca

TOURS
www.komododragontravel.com
www.komodoflorestour.com
www.komodotours.com
www.steppestravel.co.uk

FIND OUT MORE
www.komododragonfacts.com
www.komodonationalpark.org

 Move if a Komodo dragon heads towards you

 Go trekking with an open wound or if you are menstruating

MACAWS
AT A SALT LICK

"*I*magine **floating down a river** in darkness, torchlight glancing on the trees. As dawn approaches, early **mottled light** makes the salt lick glow, a **soft pink**. Above the background hum of the jungle a **happy cackling** signals the arrival of the first macaws. Steadily they're joined by more, until **there are hundreds**, perching on the clay and nibbling bite-size chunks. Then, without a hint of warning, a hawk soars overhead. Like a giant party popper there's an **explosion of colours**: sparks of reds and yellows, flashes of blue and green, as the macaws take to the air. The noise is overwhelming – a **cacophony** of squawking, squealing and **screeching**. Eventually the danger passes and the birds flock back, to resume their **manic pecking** – completely **unaware** of their human spies.

IAN WOOD

THE ENCOUNTER

Although some hides are located on land, the ultimate way to encounter macaws is from a floating catamaran hide – referred to as a 'blind'. In Peru's Manu National Park, this allows you to get as close as 20m to the clay bank. Numbers are usually limited to about a dozen people, with comfortable seating and bird identification charts to double check your sightings.

Often the smaller birds arrive first – chestnut-fronted macaws, mealy parrots and white-eyed parakeets – while larger species such as scarlet and red-and-green macaws sit in the tree tops, waiting to make sure all is safe.

Each year, thousands come to witness these festivals of colour, giving hope that the money and publicity generated from tourism will encourage governments to enforce measures to halt both the pet trade and the hunting of these birds.

▲   There are 17 species of macaw, including the military green macaw.
▶   Macaws typically mate for life and enjoy mutual grooming.
◀◀ Red-and-green macaws are one of the most numerous species seen at salt licks.

SENSITIVE WHISKERS

Sitting in a hide by a river, you might get the added bonus of observing the largest otter in the world. Giant river otters are busy, sociable animals that live in family groups and communicate through whining squeals and high-pitched hums. Sweeps of their powerful tails propel their velvety bodies through the river and they're capable of diving to depths of up to 18m. With ears and nostrils closed to keep them watertight, they can stay under water for up to eight minutes on each breath.

DETOX

Why macaws and parrots visit salt licks is not still not fully understood. The common theory is that they supplement their diet with minerals from the soil, but there is another possibility. Although many mammals and birds are seed dispersers – eating fruit, but not harming the actual seeds – parrots and macaws are seed predators: they eat and destroy the pips. As an aid to plant survival, the seeds of many fruits are laden with bitter-tasting toxins, so it's thought that by licking the clay, the birds might be helping to neutralise these poisons.

IN BRIEF

SIZE
30–100cm/150g–1.5kg, depending on the species

STATUS
3 critically endangered; 4 endangered;
10 threatened or vulnerable

HOW
Hide

WHO
12+

WHEN & WHERE
1 ECUADOR
• Napa Wildlife Centre, Yasunì National Park (Aug–Dec)

2 PERU
• Blanquillo Clay Lick, Manu National Park (Jun–Nov)
• Colpa Colorado, Tambopata Reserve (Jun–Oct)

TOURS
www.manu-wildlife-center.com
www.napowildlifecenter.com
www.tambopatatours.com

FIND OUT MORE
www.macawlanding.org
www.parrots.org

 Enjoy the sense of anticipation

 Forget to take binoculars

GETTING CLOSE TO
MINIBEASTS

We're a fickle bunch, us humans. There are some creatures which we all like — dolphins, orangutans and tigers. Then there are the ones we tend to fear — snakes and sharks would fit the bill — and plenty more that we just ignore.

Any wildlife encounter can be enhanced by keeping watch for smaller things along the way. Take tropical rainforests. Lurking under leaves, a dazzling range of insects hides from the dangers of the jungle. Like staring at the stars on a dark night, the longer you look, the more you'll see. In one study, a single square metre of leaf litter, when analysed, turned up 50 species of ants alone. In fact, as humans we are outnumbered by an overwhelming 1.5 million ants for every person or, more succinctly, the total biomass of ants is estimated to equal that of humans. Just to watch a column of ants on the march is to be in awe of their powers of organisation.

Spiders play the numbers game, too. A staggering 34,000 different species have been recorded to date – and estimates put the actual number at over 70,000. With odds like that, it's feasible that you could be looking at an undiscovered specimen crawling in the forest or hanging in its web. Almost all spiders immobilise their prey with a venomous substance, but fortunately only about a dozen carry

LEFT Praying mantis are the only insect capable of rotating their heads by 180 degrees.
CENTRE Robber flies are predators of many other insects, often catching them in mid-air.
RIGHT Male giraffe-necked weevils use their extended necks to fight with rivals to win mating rights.

any threat to humans. Even the bite of the infamous tarantula is only harmful to humans who happen to be allergic to their venom.

While some spiders, such as the ladybird spider, appear to mimic their minibeast brethren, other creatures choose out-and-out disguise. Blending in perfectly with their surroundings, **praying mantis** simply wait for food to stumble accidentally into their path. Capable of rotating their alien-like heads through 180 degrees, and with acute eyesight, they gorge on other insects, snapping them up with lightning-fast movements of their forelegs. And there's worse. The female praying mantis can be an evil seductress, luring a male to mate and then feasting on his head.

With long-hinged necks and bright-red wing covers, disguise is no part of the armoury of **giraffe-necked weevils**, which make their home in the forests of Madagascar. Only the males have the full extended necks, looking like miniature toy cranes. Wielding them like weapons, they engage in battles with their rivals where the winner gets mating privileges. Females are the home makers, using their smaller necks to roll a leaf tube nest where they lay a single egg. Giraffe-necked weevils don't hunt other insects, preferring a simple diet of leaves from the giraffe beetle tree, which is indigenous to Madagascar.

Occasionally, insects gather in such large numbers that the effect is spectacular. Each summer, the forest-fringed rivers that meander through the Hortobágy region of Hungary stage one of the greatest insect shows on earth when giant or **Tisza mayflies** swarm. The flies take up to three years to develop in their larval stage, but when conditions are right – usually late afternoon in mid June – millions emerge en masse for an insect orgy. Why? They have just three hours to mate before they die.

In summertime, millions of Tisza mayflies swarm in Hortobágy, Hungary.

LION ENCOUNTERS
ON A WALKING SAFARI

"*I've seen lions closer – much closer – but now there's no metallic barrier of a vehicle. We're crouched down, **hardly daring to breathe**, as just **metres away** three lions gorge – blood smeared across their faces. They've already half devoured the zebra – ribcage torn apart; two hoofed feet splayed out wide. The largest of the trio has a dark **rugged mane** that frames his **battle-scarred face**; using one paw, he holds the carcass steady, tearing off another lump of flesh. But suddenly his body language changes. Sniffing the air, he turns and **stares straight at us**. Next to me, our guide grips his rifle with a vigour that only adds to the **tension**. For a few seconds there's a stand off. Then, almost **nonchalantly**, the big male returns to the matter in hand. **We're dismissed**.*"

IAN WOOD

Highly distinctive with their manes and often scarred faces, male lions can patrol vast territories up to 250km².

THE ENCOUNTER

Although the most reliable way of seeing lions is from a safari vehicle, encountering them on foot adds an entirely different dimension. Walking through the dry savanna, keeping careful watch for footprints, scat markings and flattened areas of grass: you're in their territory, on their terms; it's heart-racing stuff.

While you can never guarantee lion encounters on a walking safari, a good guide will know where to look, especially if there's been a recent kill, and will help to explain their habitat. Should you find a pride of lions, the chances are that they will be sleeping or resting, which they do for up to 20 hours a day. If they spot you coming they will often slink away long before you're near, but approach silently downwind and you can sometimes get as close as 20 metres. Lions are extremely well camouflaged and it is possible to stumble across one without warning. If you do, then back off slowly – but never run from a big cat.

ANT LION

When walking in African savanna you will sometimes spot small funnel-like patterns in the sand. Measuring about 5cm across, they hide another fearsome – albeit miniature –predator-in-waiting. With a small fat body and a pair of oversized mandibles, the ant lion is the larval stage of a flying insect. As ants and other insects stumble upon the trap, they lose their footing and slide down into the waiting jaws beneath. The ant lion consumes its prey by sucking it dry, before discarding the carcass and patiently waiting for its next victim.

▲ Seeing lions on foot is a completely different experience to observing them from the safety of a safari vehicle.

◤ Lion cubs are raised not just by their mothers, but by other females within the pride.

FAMILY BONDS

Lacking the speed of the cheetah and the stealth of a leopard forces lions to rely on teamwork. Typically, a pride will comprise about five adult females, their cubs and one or more adult males, but occasionally groups can number up to 40 individuals. Females form the basis of lion society, remaining with their birth pride forever and forming powerful alliances. But life isn't so simple for the males, which are forced to leave their family at about two years old for an uncertain nomadic future. Even if they make it to adulthood they will need to fight for their right to join a new group, with many a male dying in these battles to acquire or defend a pride.

ETHICS OF 'WALKING WITH LIONS'

There are several companies in Africa that offer opportunities to walk with and handle lion cubs, but these experiences are a world apart from walking safaris. Often billed as captive breeding programmes, they usually proclaim that when the cubs are bigger they will be released into the wild. The problem is that a constant supply of lion cubs is needed and some are then sold on to hunting estates where people pay to kill them. I've not met a single lion conservationist who isn't opposed to this practice, so as tempting as it is, avoid these projects and take your chances on a lion encounter in the wild.

IN BRIEF

SIZE
1.4–2m/120–190kg

STATUS
Vulnerable

HOW
Walking safari

WHO
16+

WHEN & WHERE
1 BOTSWANA
• Okavango Delta (all year)

2 KENYA
• Maasai Mara National Reserve (all year; rainy season Apr–May & Nov)

3 TANZANIA
• Selous Game Reserve (Jun–Feb)
• Serengeti National Park (all year; rainy season Apr–May & Nov)

4 ZAMBIA
• Kafue National Park (Jun–Oct)
• Lower Zambezi National Park (May–Oct)
• North & South Luangwa National Parks (Jun–Oct)

5 ZIMBABWE
• Hwange National Park (all year)
• Mana Pools National Park (Jun–Oct)

TOURS
www.expertafrica.com
www.rainbowtours.co.uk
www.wildlifeworldwide.com
www.worldbigcatsafaris.com

FIND OUT MORE
www.african-lion.org
www.lionconservation.org

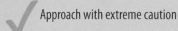 Approach with extreme caution   Never run from a big cat

CHEETAH
SAFARI

*O*n the edge of the herd, an impala has noticed something: **tense**, ears twitching. Slowly, we drive in the direction of **its gaze**, scanning the savanna until we spot the cheetah, partly camouflaged by a tree – **transfixed** on its prey. There's a burst of activity as it darts across to the next bush, only to resume its **silent vigil**. We watch as this pattern is repeated until the cheetah is **close enough for action**. Then, a lengthy pause; the **suspense** is almost suffocating. My loyalties are divided, like a silent witness choosing to ignore the pending crime. Suddenly, exploding from cover, it tears across the scrub – a **blur of fluid speed**. The antelope stands no chance. **Pouncing** on its back, the cheetah wrestles it to the ground, scattering dust into the arid air.

IAN WOOD

THE ENCOUNTER

Cheetahs are famous for being the fastest land animal, running at speeds of up to 120km/h. Even though you're more likely to see them resting in tall grasses, or near bushes and larger shrubs, getting close to a wild cheetah on foot is an unlikely scenario. This is one occasion when you need an open-topped game vehicle.

Although cheetahs are mainly solitary, groups of males will sometimes hunt in a gang, enabling them to catch larger prey such as wildebeest and zebra. But being built for speed has a drawback; cheetahs are too slender to fight off other predators and cannot defend their kill. Thus daylight hours are your best chance of seeing them in action, when rivals such as lions and hyenas are resting. Or head out on an evening game drive – searchlight scanning the bush, sounds of scavengers calling in the void.

SPOT THE DIFFERENCE

It's easy to confuse a cheetah with a leopard when it's lying in the grass, but there are obvious differences. Instead of rosette-shaped spots, cheetahs have single larger ones, like thumbprints dotted on their fur. Their heads are much smaller in relation to their bodies, too, keeping them streamlined for spurts of speed. And on either side of their nose, two black lines run down – like teardrops from the corners of their eyes.

Individual cats can be identified by their unique markings, which can aid the study and conservation of these cats. If you photograph a cheetah anywhere in Tanzania, make a note of where and when you saw it

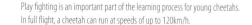
▲   Play fighting is an important part of the learning process for young cheetahs.
◄◄   In full flight, a cheetah can run at speeds of up to 120km/h.

and send your image to the Cheetah Watch Campaign (www.tanzaniacarnivores.org); in Zambia, a similar project is run by the Zambian Carnivore Programme (www.zambiacarnivores.org).

KEEP IT IN THE FAMILY

Cheetahs are the most threatened of all Africa's cats but the reasons lie unexpectedly far back in time, when they came remarkably close to extinction. By studying their enzymes, scientists think that about 10,000 years ago, fewer than seven individuals were left. The cheetahs' only means of survival was by interbreeding, leaving them with a tiny gene pool. This lack of genetic diversity has severely weakened them as a species, with low rates of reproduction, poor sperm counts and high rates of infant mortality.

IN BRIEF

SIZE
1.5m/40–70kg

STATUS
Vulnerable

HOW
Game drive

WHO
Often 8+

WHEN & WHERE
1 BOTSWANA
• Okavango Delta (Jun–Dec)
• Central Kalahari Game Reserve (Nov–Apr)

2 KENYA Maasai Mara National Reserve (all year; rainy season Apr–May & Nov)

3 NAMIBIA
• Etosha National Park (May–Oct)

4 SOUTH AFRICA
• Phinda Game Reserve (Jun–Sep)
• Kgalagadi Transfrontier National Park (Jan–May)
• Tswalu Kalahari Game Reserve (all year)

5 TANZANIA
• Ndutu Plains, Ngorongoro Conservation Area (Dec–Apr)
• Ruaha National Park (Jun–Oct)

6 ZAMBIA
• Busanga Plains, Kafue National Park (Jul–Oct)

TOURS
www.expertafrica.com
www.rainbowtours.co.uk
www.wildlifeworldwide.com
www.worldbigcatsafaris.com

FIND OUT MORE
www.cheetahbotswana.com
www.cheetah.co.za
www.cheetah.org

 Remain absolutely silent

 Confuse them with a leopard

AFRICAN
HORSERIDING SAFARI

Horseriding is arguably the ultimate way to see wildlife in Africa. Spending up to six hours a day in the saddle, riding through a variety of habitats, at one with nature.

Most animals and birds have no natural fear of horses and don't see the human astride them as a separate entity. The result? An invisibility cloak that affords enviably close encounters – provided that you know what you're doing.

Imagine setting out on horseback in the cool of early morning with just the sound of hoofs and chirping birds. Each day will vary enormously, from walking along dried-up river beds and hurdling fallen trees, to exhilarating gallops alongside zebra across open savanna. Or witnessing normally skittish **giraffe** calmly watching as you roam amongst their herd.

Even potentially dangerous animals such as rhino react very differently to horses and, providing you approach in the correct manner, will sometimes let you get surprisingly close. It should go without saying that you need to heed your guide's advice, but often the best tactic is to advance slowly in a zigzag style. This is one encounter where silence isn't golden; it's usually best to keep talking to get the rhinos accustomed to your presence. When they first notice you, letting your horse stop and graze will reassure the rhinos that you pose no threat. Once they resume feeding you can repeat this pattern – edging cautiously forward. Find yourself just metres away from a group of rhinos – facing you like a line of opposing tanks – and you will probably feel your heart racing, while your horse remains unflustered, calmly chomping on the grass.

Elephants need special attention, particularly in areas where poachers have used horses for their trade. Always approach slowly and silently, keeping careful watch for changes in their body language. If a bull or matriarch elephant shakes its head – ears flapping angrily – then heed the warning and turn away before it charges.

No matter what you encounter, any good horse–human partnership is based on understanding and trust. As an experienced rider, you can use your horse's heightened senses to help you spot wildlife and stay alert to hidden dangers, ensuring that you get the most out of your time in the saddle.

▶ Riding on horseback can offer close encounters with even skittish animals like giraffes.

IN BRIEF

It's essential that you are an experienced rider. This includes rising to the trot, controlling your horse at a canter and being able to gallop out of trouble. If you can ride, but don't do so on a regular basis, make sure you are fit enough to meet the physical demands of several days in the saddle. Typically you will be in a small group of up to eight riders, but as many horseback safaris set up camp each night, they can sometimes accommodate non-riding partners who may get their own unique off-road safari via the support vehicle.

WHEN
All year

WHERE
1 BOTSWANA
• Limpopo Valley
• Okavango Delta

2 KENYA
• Samangua Valley

3 NAMIBIA
• Namib-Naukluft Mountains

4 SOUTH AFRICA
• Waterberg Mountains

5 TANZANIA
• Grumeti Reserve

6 ZAMBIA
• Shiwa Ng'andu Estate

7 ZIMBABWE
• Mana Pools National Park

TOUR OPERATORS
www.inthesaddle.com
www.rideafrica.com
www.rideworldwide.co.uk

Only experienced riders are accepted on horseback safaris and a good level of fitness is required for long days in the saddle.

TRACKING
LEOPARD
BY 4x4

*"It looks like a comfortable spot to take a nap. Body **draped** along the branch, limbs hanging down on either side, her **mottled coat** is further **dappled by the sun**, glinting through the leaves. Motionless – well, nearly. Like a gentle tide, her body swells and falls on every sleepy breath. The lower lip is squashed by the **weight of her jaw** and droops slightly, revealing two sharp teeth. A single drop of saliva forms and falls onto the **dusty savanna** below. **Lazily**, she half opens one eye and looks at us, but even that seems too much effort. Her eyelid sinks back down; I think I can even hear her **purring**."*

IAN WOOD

THE ENCOUNTER

Unless you're very lucky and find a leopard with her cubs, you will probably meet these solitary animals alone. Leopards prefer areas with plenty of trees, which provide cover when hunting, as well as acting as a refuge from threats such as lions and hyenas.

A traditional safari vehicle is best: open-topped for maximum visibility and with good spotlights; while leopards are often seen in trees during the day, to watch them hunting you will need to be on a night drive. Typically, when they're at rest, you approach the tree – engine ticking – and most leopards will just stare back, unfazed by your arrival, or by your camera. When they're hunting, though, they're focused on their prey and you need to keep absolute silence.

Your guide will follow a number of clues when tracking leopards, including paw prints – males' are larger and have a slightly shorter distance between their toes and pads than females' – and scratch marks on trees.

A FLASH OF COLOUR

Among the trees favoured by leopards you'll see an array of birdlife, including the woodland kingfisher. Between September and November, these intra-African migrants arrive in southern African to breed, returning to central Africa by April. Distinctive in their black, white and turquoise livery, with a smart crimson bill, they are often seen perching on a dead branch, or swooping down to snare an insect snack. Aggressively territorial, they defend their patch with raucous calls and displays of wing fanning.

▲ Your best chance of seeing a leopard during the day is to look up into the branches of a tree.

◥ Leopards will often haul their prey up into a tree for safe keeping.

◀◀ Being nocturnal, leopards spend most of the day resting in trees or thick undergrowth.

  SAVANNA

SLEEK & STRONG

Leopards are cunning, stealthy hunters, capable of catching a diverse range of prey including fish, reptiles, impala, gazelle and even larger animals such as young zebra, giraffe and wildebeest. Mainly hunting at night, they use their acute hearing and sight to stalk their victim before pouncing and swiftly despatching it with a bite to the throat. Immensely strong, they will usually haul the carcass – sometimes larger than themselves – high up into a tree for protection from scavengers.

IN BRIEF

SIZE
1.3–1.9m/30–80kg

STATUS
Near threatened

HOW
4x4 game drive

WHO
Often 8+

WHEN & WHERE

1 BOTSWANA
- Chobe National Park (Apr–Oct)
- Footsteps, Selinda & Linyanti Wildlife Reserves (Apr–Oct)
- Vumbura, Chitabe, Moremi & Chief's Island Reserves (all year)

2 KENYA
- Maasai Mara National Reserve (all year; rainy season Apr, May & Nov)

3 NAMIBIA
- Etosha National Park (May–Oct)

4 SOUTH AFRICA
- Sabi Sands Game Reserve (Jun–Oct)

5 TANZANIA
- Serengeti National Park (all year; rainy season Apr, May & Nov)

6 ZAMBIA
- Kafue National Park (May–Oct)
- Lower Zambezi National Park (Jun–Oct)
- North & South Luangwa National Parks (Jun–Oct)

7 ZIMBABWE
- Matobo National Park (Apr–Oct)

TOURS
www.expertafrica.com
www.rainbowtours.co.uk
www.steppestravel.co.uk
www.worldbigcatsafaris.com

FIND OUT MORE
www.capeleopard.org.za
www.leopardcon.co.za

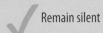 Remain silent

 Make any sudden movements

ELEPHANTS
ON A WALKING SAFARI

"*My guide leads the way – rifle casually slung over his shoulder, twigs snapping underfoot. Reaching the waterhole we sit and wait, **sheltering from the heat** under the umbrella of an acacia tree. On the far side, a herd of five elephants approaches with **silent lumbering steps**, trunks swaying side to side. Just short of the pool the matriarch stops, gently flapping her ears, **examining** us. Satisfied, she leads the way forward, **giant feet** squelching in the mud, to take **great slurps** of water – and spray jets across her leathery skin. Her young calf tries to do the same, but its wobbly trunk doesn't quite oblige, so mum takes over, **drenching it** in a drizzle of fine mist.*

IAN WOOD

THE ENCOUNTER

Elephants are one of the most impressive animals on earth: moving purposefully yet with almost dainty steps, purveying an earthy sense of dignity and wisdom. Watch elephants from a game vehicle and there's always the safety of the accelerator, but nothing compares to seeing them on foot. Standing in their territory you'll feel insignificant, dwarfed by both their size and their sheer strength.

How close you can get to an elephant on foot depends on the individual animals and the location, but it can be less than 30 metres. You may even be lucky enough to find a spot close to a waterhole where you can observe a whole family coming down for a morning bathe. Yet elephants are surprisingly sensitive so it's vital to approach with caution while keeping a careful watch on their body language. Initially, a wary elephant will stand tall – head raised and ears spread. Think of this as a first level of alert, perhaps because it's just noticed you. If they feel threatened, perhaps because there's a young calf present, or if a male is in musth, elephants will start to jerk and toss their heads, ears slapping on their faces. An elephant that rolls up its trunk and then unfurls it with a loud trumpet blast is very nervous and could become a serious threat. In this state, it might rip up and throw branches or even small trees. Such warnings should be sufficient to convince you to back off, slowly and calmly, avoiding the situation where an angry elephant charges, roaring its disapproval. Signs of uncertainty preceding a charge can sometimes be an indication of a mock charge, as opposed to a real one – but don't ever count on it.

▲   Always keep a careful eye on an elephant's body language and back off at the first sign of any stress.
◀◀   Using their trunks, elephants can suck up about ten litres of water before spraying it in their mouths or showering their bodies.

ELEPHANT SHREW

Everyone is familiar with the 'big five' but walking through the African savanna affords opportunities to encounter members of the 'little five' too. The elephant shrew is a small, insect-eating mammal which gets its name from the long flexible trunk that it uses to sniff out prey. Looking like a bizarre cross between a mouse and an elephant, it's a busy animal – darting about in search of food. Despite the name, they aren't in fact shrews; recent evidence suggests that they belong to a group of African mammals that does indeed include elephants, as well as sea cows and aardvarks.

MEET THE FAMILY

It's a humbling experience, seeing elephants on foot; they exude a combination of power, peace and intelligence. Maybe it's because they've roamed the earth for over 50 million years – which makes our mere 200,000 seem like an evolutionary blink. From fossil evidence we know that over 300 species of elephants once existed, but today we're left with three:

AFRICAN BUSH ELEPHANT
Famous for their large ears which help to dissipate heat, these are the world's largest land mammals. Remarkably adaptable, they roam the grassy plains, bush lands and even deserts of more than 30 countries in sub-Saharan Africa.

AFRICAN FOREST ELEPHANT
Through DNA testing, scientists now consider African forest elephants to be a unique species rather than a subspecies of their bush cousins. Living in the equatorial forests of central and western Africa, they look quite different, too – smaller and darker with straight thin tusks and rounded ears.

ASIAN ELEPHANT
Smaller than either of their African relatives, Asian elephants survive in 12 countries, including India, Sri Lanka, Thailand, Indonesia and Malaysia. Their skin is less wrinkled and usually freckled in appearance, especially on their trunks. In northeast Borneo there is a population of pygmy elephants which are a third smaller again and believed to be a subspecies.

▶   Like African elephants, Asian elephants make trumpet calls both to communicate and to warn potential predators to stay away.
▶▶ Baby elephants are totally dependent on their mothers for up to five years.

FAMILY BONDS

Female elephants are profoundly social creatures living in tight-knit herds. Setting the pace and direction, the matriarch leads her clan in search of food and water. When she stops to feed, you'll notice the rest of the herd spread out slightly and eat too – but never straying far. When threatened, they cluster around the matriarch, protecting their calves in the middle of the group. New arrivals are doted on with great care and female offspring will remain in this group for their entire lives. A bull elephant, however, is shunned after adolescence, to prevent him from mating with the younger females. Although males occasionally form bachelor herds, they tend to lead a solitary life with annual periods of heightened sexual activity called musth. Dribbling a trail of strong-smelling urine and making frequent mating calls, bull elephants can be highly aggressive in this state and need to be given a wide berth.

WELL HUNG

You'd expect an elephant to be suitably endowed and it is: at up to two metres long, theirs is the largest penis of any land animal. But even more impressive is their ability to control these tools. When mating, their massive bodies don't afford the same degree of movement compared with smaller animals so a prehensile penis is a necessity. It would be a shame to waste this extra asset and elephants sometimes use their manly organs for much more mundane tasks: swatting flies, scratching skin and even acting as an extra temporary limb to steady themselves.

IN BRIEF

SIZE
African bush, to 7.5m long, 4m high/6,000kg
African forest, to 4m long, 3m high/5,000kg
Asian, to 3.5m long, 3m high/5,000kg

STATUS
African bush & forest, vulnerable; Asian, endangered

HOW
Walking safari

WHO
16+

WHEN & WHERE
African elephant

1 BOTSWANA
• Footsteps across the Delta, Okavango Delta (Mar–Nov)

2 CENTRAL AFRICAN REPUBLIC
• Dzanga–Sangha National Park (Nov–Apr)

3 GABON
• Loango National Park (all year)

4 GHANA
• Mole National Park (all year)

5 KENYA
• Maasai Mara National Reserve (all year; rainy season Apr–May & Nov)
• Tsavo National Park (all year; rainy season Apr–May)

6 SOUTH AFRICA
• Kruger National Park (all year)

7 TANZANIA
• Selous Game Reserve (Jun–Feb)
• Serengeti National Park (all year; rainy season Apr–May & Nov)
• Tarangire National Park (all year)

8 ZAMBIA (Jun–Oct)
• Lower Zambezi National Park
• North & South Luangwa National Parks

9 ZIMBABWE
• Hwange National Park (May–Oct)
• Mana Pools National Park (May–Oct)

Asian elephant
10 INDIA
• Periyar National Park (all year)

11 MALAYSIA
• Danum Valley, Borneo (all year; rainy season Nov–Apr)

12 SRI LANKA
• Uda Walawe National Park (May–Sep)

TOURS
www.africaonfoot.com
www.expertafrica.com
www.rainbowtours.co.uk
www.wildernessjourneys.com

FIND OUT MORE
www.elephantconservation.org
www.elephantfamily.org
www.elephanttrust.org

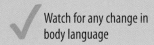 Watch for any change in body language

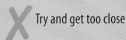 Try and get too close

THE
WILDEBEEST
MIGRATION

"*Sitting in a jeep, quietly overlooking the Mara River in the northern Serengeti, there are no other vehicles in sight. The **distant noise** of lowing grows nearer and, slowly, **engulfs us.** As we wait, the dust in the air grows heavy and hot. Then it starts. First a trickle, then **a cascade**: grey-brown wildebeest **hurtle** down the steep banks to lunge into the fast-flowing river. Huge crocs catch a few – it's their annual time of plenty – but most flail and ultimately **power through**, trampling one another in their **desperation** to cross. Eventually, after much sound and **fury**, it's over. A few haven't made it, but most walk away as if nothing happened. The lowing gradually recedes; it's quiet again.*"

CHRIS McINTYRE
www.expertafrica.com
EXPERT AFRICA

THE ENCOUNTER

The numbers in this cast are staggering: one-and-a-half million wildebeest, half-a-million Thompson's gazelle and a few hundred-thousand zebra and impala – all rumbling across the savanna. A mass migration on this scale never goes unnoticed; hungry predators such as lions, leopards and crocodiles are ready to pounce on easy prey.

CIRCLE OF LIFE

Although the exact timing of the annual wildebeest migration is dependent on seasonal rains, it usually follows a well-defined pattern. The circle of life begins in January when herds of wildebeest gather in the southern Serengeti. After rain, these abundant plains offer the perfect place for the animals to calve.

GRANDSTAND VIEW

A plethora of safari lodges exists along the migration route, with the most popular locations providing views over the Grumeti and Mara river crossings. Mobile safari camps also spring up to take advantage of specific migration hotspots, depending on the individual year. Or take a hot-air-balloon ride to get an aerial view of the greatest wildlife migration on earth. You won't be disappointed.

▲   For a bird's-eye view of the great migration, take to the air in a hot-air balloon.
◣   Crocodiles lurk in these rivers – waiting for easy prey.
◀◀ It's a free-for-all when wildebeest cross rivers, often trampling one another.

  SAVANNA

Thousands are born every day, swelling the numbers with up to half-a-million new arrivals in just three or four weeks.

By March or April, life has changed. Parched by the sun, the dry savanna can no longer sustain these massive herds. Sweeping north and west to the grassier plains and woodlands of Serengeti's western corridor provides them with food. But time waits for no herbivore and by June the savanna here turns yellow too. Usually the herds will split, with one group trundling further west and the other heading north, thundering onwards and upwards to face their first serious obstacle – the bottleneck of the Grumeti River. High densities congregate on the southern banks, until the braver ones decide to cross – triggering a stampede that draws crocodiles to the surface to pick off the weaker animals.

Yet this is just a dress rehearsal for the ultimate challenge: the mighty Mara River. Between August and October the herds regroup, torn between the dangers of the crossing and the fresh grazing beyond. Once again, it takes a few hardy souls to take the first steps, sparking off a mass exodus down the steep riverbanks, with many to be trampled, drowned or simply picked off by the crocs.

Come October, the northern savanna is packed with survivors, but – stalked by predators night and day – they've no time to relax. Soon, the rains have started in the south and they must begin their long journey back through Tanzania: ready to give birth again, before setting out on an eternal lap of honour.

IN BRIEF

SIZE
Up to 1.4m/250kg

STATUS
Least concern

HOW
Jeep, lodge, hot-air balloon

WHO
Hot-air balloon 7+

WHEN & WHERE
1 KENYA
• Maasai Mara National Reserve (Sep–Oct)

2 TANZANIA
• Serengeti National Park, northeast (Nov)
• Serengeti National Park, east (Dec)
• Southern Serengeti & Ngorongoro Conservation Area (Jan–Mar)
• Serengeti National Park, Seronera (Apr)
• Serengeti National Park, western corridor (May)
• Serengeti National Park, western corridor & Grumeti Game Reserve (Jun–Jul)
• Serengeti National Park, northwest (Aug–Sep)

TOURS
www.expertafrica.com (see page 178)
www.kenyamasaimaraadventuresafaris.com
www.naturalhighsafaris.com
www.wildlifeworldwide.com

 Choose your place and time with care

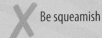 Be squeamish

TRACKING
AFRICAN RHINO
ON FOOT

"There are no jeep tracks, just **endless savanna**. Following our guide's hand signals, we edge forward in single file until he stops and points. Crouching behind a bush, I can see five white rhinos – folds of **armour-plated skin** – about 50m away, chomping on the grass. After a pause, we're ushered on – slowly, **silently**, step by careful step; it reminds me of creeping up on someone in a childhood game. But this is **serious**, rhino are **dangerous** beasts. Another ten metres and it's close enough; we crouch again. There's a feeling of **tension** and **vulnerability** as they stop munching and raise their heads – acutely aware of our presence – just uncertain of exactly where we are."

IAN WOOD

White rhinos are more sociable than black rhinos, sometimes forming groups of females and sub-adults.

THE ENCOUNTER

Tracking rhinos on foot is a specialist job. Easily startled – and with notoriously poor eyesight – they are capable of charging at over 50km/h. Black rhinos are the more aggressive of the two species, with a tendency to attack anything perceived as a threat – they've even been known to assault trees and other harmless objects by mistake. In a small group (six or fewer), you'll be accompanied be armed guides experienced in finding these animals. Whereas white rhinos are often seen in a small herd, their black relatives are solitary creatures – apart from mothers with a calf. Hearing and smell are their most acute senses, so it's vital to stay quiet, approach downwind and follow your guide's instructions at all times.

BLACK & WHITE

The difference between black and white rhinos has nothing to do with colour. The confusion began when Dutch settlers named the 'weit mond rhino', which translates as 'wide mouthed'. Not being great linguists, the English thought they were saying 'white' – and the name stuck.

The slightly larger white rhino has a wide, square mouth designed for grazing, whereas the black rhino has a pointed, hook-shaped upper lip that it uses to eat other vegetation, including shoots, leaves and even fruit.

▲   To tell the difference between white and black rhinos look at the head. White rhinos have a broader mouth whereas the black species has a distinctive hook-shaped upper lip.

  SAVANNA

RHINOCEROS BEETLE

Down at ground level in the Africa, savanna is one of the strongest creatures in the world: the rhinoceros beetle. Capable of lifting up to 850 times their own weight, the males boast two horns protruding from their heads, just like their namesakes. Disturb them and you'll hear a loud hissing squeak, but it's just a bluff – they pose no threat at all. If you crouch down close, you'll see their abdomens rhythmically moving in time with the squeaks.

COLLAPSE IN NUMBERS

Black rhinos were once the most numerous of the world's five species, topping 60,000 in the late 1960s. Yet within barely 20 years, poachers despatched over 96%, and by 1993 fewer than 2,500 animals remained. Since then, intensive anti-poaching efforts have helped to stabilise numbers, with populations even slowly increasing in some areas. Although the illegal trade in rhinoceros horn still poses a significant threat, white rhinos have fared much better in recent times. Today about 15,000 roam in the wild, a remarkable comeback from a population that fell below a hundred in 1895.

IN BRIEF

SIZE
Black rhino up to 3.5m/1,400kg
White rhino up to 4.5m/2,700kg

STATUS
Black rhino critically endangered
White rhino near threatened

HOW
On foot

WHO
16+

WHEN
All year unless specified

WHERE
1 BOTSWANA
• Chief's Island, Okavango Delta (May–Oct)
• Khama Rhino Sanctuary (May–Oct)

2 KENYA
• Ol Pejeta Conservancy

3 NAMIBIA
• Desert Rhino Camp, Damaraland
• Ongava Reserve
• Mundulea Nature Reserve

4 SOUTH AFRICA
• Tswalu Game Reserve

5 SWAZILAND
• Mkhaya Game Reserve

6 ZAMBIA
• Mosi-oa-Tunya National Park

7 ZIMBABWE
• Matobo Hills National Park (Apr–Oct)
• Matusadona National Park (Jun–Oct)

TOURS
www.expertafrica.com
www.rainbowtours.co.uk
www.steppestravel.co.uk

FIND OUT MORE
www.savingrhinos.org
www.savetherhino.org

✓ Follow your guide's instructions   ✗ Make any sudden noise

EXPEDITION IN
SNOW LEOPARD
TERRITORY

"*My guide saw it first, excitedly pointing towards the mountain slope, beaming with pride. Initially, it looked like a rock protruding from the snow, a dot on this* **pristine white landscape** *that towers up towards the sky. But staring through my spotting scope affords me an* **intimate view**. *She might be 600m away – maybe more – but with this magnification I can even see her* **steamy breath**. *With the circular barrel pressed against my face, I stalk her every move.* **Stealthily** *picking a path across the wilderness,* **rosettes of smoky grey** *rippling at every move, she sweeps her thick, oversized tail behind. It is dusk before I lose sight of her, and the temperature is plummeting, but that sensuous movement, those rosettes, remain* **imprinted** *on my mind.*"

IAN WOOD

THE ENCOUNTER

Trekking through the high central mountains of Asia is inspiring in its own right, the crisp thin air cleansing your lungs with every breath. That's just as well, for on any trek in search of snow leopards, a sighting is a bonus. Even local people rarely see these elusive cats.

The trek is like an expedition, sometimes camping in temperatures below freezing; at others sleeping in homestays. By day you track, hunting for scat markings, gleaning information from villagers; if their livestock is being stalked, that's a lead to follow. With the naked eye you'll be lucky to get a good view of a snow leopard, as most will be over 500m away, but a spotting scope, an essential part of your kit, will be supplied by your tour company.

HUMAN-LEOPARD CONFLICT

Scarcely 6,000 snow leopards remain in the wild and their biggest threat is from humans, who have long since hunted them for their fur. But people also deplete their food sources by killing the prey animals on which they feed. When their natural food isn't available, snow leopards will kill domestic sheep and goats, causing hardship for local communities.

Snow leopards are native to the high central mountains of Asia. Their range extends through Afghanistan, Bhutan, China, India, Kazakhstan, the Kyrgyz Republic, Mongolia, Nepal, Pakistan, Russia, Tajikistan –

▲ Most people who live near snow leopard territory have never seen these elusive cats.
◀◀ The snow leopard's paws have fur-covered pads to help with insulation and aid traction.

BLUE SHEEP

As you scan the surrounding landscape, the chances are that any signs of movement will be from blue sheep — which are neither blue, nor in fact sheep. With backward sweeping horns, they are more closely related to goats, and are perfect prey for snow leopards. You may also spot another source of prey: the wild yak. With shaggy coats, small legs and hollow horns, they are among the hardiest animals in the world, aided by an internal central-heating system fuelled by the fermentation of digested plants in their intestines!

but it is in India that you have the best chance of seeing them. In 2001, a homestay programme was established in India's Ladakh region, providing a direct incentive to preserve wildlife and helping to offset losses from livestock predation. Jobs have also been created by training people as guides and running cafés and solar showers along the most popular trekking routes. To date, over a hundred households in more than 40 villages have a financial stake in snow leopard conservation.

MOUNTAIN GHOST

Few Nepalese people have ever seen a snow leopard, giving rise to the local nickname 'mountain ghost'. To gain a better understanding of these secretive cats, the Snow Leopard Conservancy has enlisted the help of local schoolchildren. Working in pairs, pupils have been trained to install and monitor digital camera traps, with the data being used to provide a better estimate of the remaining numbers in this region.

IN BRIEF

SIZE
1.2–1.5m/30–55kg

STATUS
Endangered

HOW
Trekking

WHO
18+

WHEN
Feb–Mar

WHERE
INDIA
• Ladakh

TOURS
www.biosphere-expeditions.org
www.indiafootprints.com
www.steppestravel.co.uk
www.worldbigcatsafaris.com

FIND OUT MORE
www.snowleopard.org
www.snowleopardconservancy.org
www.snowleopardhimalayas.org

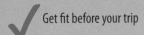 Get fit before your trip   Expect to see a snow leopard up close

TRACKING
WOLVES
ON FOOT

*First light has washed this icy landscape with an **eerie blush**. Armed with a flask of hot coffee, I'm waiting by a frozen lake, **scanning the wilderness** for any signs of movement. I know they're out there; I can hear them howling – like a distant **canine choir**. Then, a **shifty shadow** emerges from the trees. The wolf stops, scans the landscape and ventures into the open. Through my binoculars I count as the rest of the pack – five more wolves – follows. The only sound I hear is the **whistling of the wind** as I watch them walk in single file, heading away from me until they become distant specks against this barren field of white.*

NATHAN VARLEY
www.wolftracker.com
The
Wild Side
Wildlife Tours

The world's largest wild canid, the grey wolf, spends most of its time roaming in search of prey.

THE ENCOUNTER

For centuries humans have hunted wolves, often to the brink of local extinction, so we can hardly blame them for doing their best to avoid man. They are most active at dawn and dusk; you'll trek by moonlight across ice-bound land, sometimes using cross-country skis or show shoes. Tracking wolves is a covert operation and it's essential to use a guide who has intimate knowledge of both the animals and their habitat. At times, you silently stalk the forests, keeping watch for footprints in the snow; at others, you'll wait in silence near open ground, scanning the area for signs of movement. Wolves are elusive, though, and even if you do find them, a decent pair of binoculars or a spotting scope is essential, as sightings can be up to a kilometre away.

ADDED BONUS

If you thought wolves were hard to find, try searching for the mysterious lynx. With thick lush fur to protect them from the cold, short bobbed tails and pointed ears, they're rarely even glimpsed before they move swiftly away. But their pugmarks are easy to recognise as — unlike wolf tracks — you'll see only their pads. This is caused by their toes spreading out from oversized paws to stop them sinking into deep snow.

▲ Packs of grey wolves average between four and nine members but can occasionally number up to 15 individuals.
◥ With its red coat and pointed ears, the Ethiopian wolf is often mistaken for a fox or jackal.

ETHIOPIAN WOLVES

Fox-like in appearance, with reddish coats and black-tipped tails, the smaller Ethiopian wolves are confined to the country's highlands. Once thought to be related to foxes or jackals, DNA testing has shown them to be a unique species, distantly linked to their grey cousins. Yet although fewer than 500 individuals remain, you may stand a better chance of seeing them than either the European or American wolves, sometimes under 30m away. The reason? Ethiopian wolves are active during the day, roaming the high-altitude plateaux in search of grass rats and giant mole rats.

HOWLING AT THE MOON

Wolves don't actually sing to the moon, yet with noses pointed skywards and a howl of such raw, primeval beauty, it's easy to see how this myth developed. Every wolf has a unique howl which allows it to communicate with other members of its pack, reunite them after hunting and warn rival groups to stay away. A wolf's howl starts off low before steadily rising in tone. Others join in at different pitches, harmonising like a human choir, which serves to make the pack sound larger than it is.

IN BRIEF

SIZE
Grey up to 1.5m /35–55kg; Ethiopian up to 1m/20kg

STATUS
Grey wolf, least concern; Ethiopian wolf, endangered

HOW
Trekking, cross-country skiing, 4x4

WHO
16+

WHEN & WHERE
1 ETHIOPIA
• Bale National Park (Nov–Mar dry season)

2 POLAND
• Bieszczady National Park (Jan–Apr)

3 ROMANIA
• Carpathian Mountains (Nov–Mar)

4 SPAIN
• Cordillera Cantabrica (Nov–Mar)

5 SWEDEN
• Bergslagen (Jan–Mar)

6 USA
Yellowstone National Park (all year)

TOURS
www.wolftracker.com (see page 178)
www.naturetrek.co.uk
www.steppestravel.co.uk
www.wildlifewilderness.com

FIND OUT MORE
www.ethiopianwolf.org
www.graywolfconservation.com

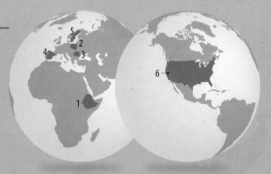

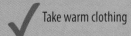 Take warm clothing

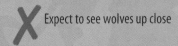 Expect to see wolves up close

SEEKING OUT THE
GIANT PANDA

"*We'd almost given up, but in the late afternoon a **fresh trail** of footprints spurred us on. Edging forward, our guide stops and crouches down. His eyes **glint with excitement** – fresh scat markings. As we walk on, the **anticipation** intensifies, until the **distinctive sound of chomping** brings us to a sudden stop. Through the **lush foliage** I can see the panda – sitting on the forest floor, munching on bamboo. He looks like a cartoon character, staring at me through **gentle eyes** encircled with two blobs of black, like badly applied make-up. **We're frozen** to the spot, but the panda, once its snack is over, moves away, **clumsily forging** through the vegetation.*"

IAN WOOD

◄ Among the most instantly recognised animals in the world, giant pandas have become an iconic symbol for conservation.

THE ENCOUNTER

Giant pandas have been a symbol of threatened wildlife since the World Wildlife Fund adopted them as its logo in 1961, but meeting one in the wild requires a combination of patience, persistence and luck. Their stronghold is the formidable wilderness that slopes down from the eastern Himalaya. Snow-clad peaks dominate the cavernous valleys; streams gush with clear cold water, and bamboos thrive.

Searching for giant pandas in this rugged countryside is an adventure in itself. Few foreign visitors explore these areas, so you'll see a way of rural life barely changed in centuries. Trekking through thick bamboo forests, often clad in mist, is a detective game. You search for clues: remains of bitten bamboo, bits of panda hair, droppings and footprints. Early starts are needed, as is a good level of physical fitness, and there is never a guarantee of a sighting. To make the most of any opportunities, silence is key; although a panda's eyesight is poor, it has an acute sense of hearing.

PANDA SANCTUARIES

The majority of visitors to China aren't prepared for such an expedition – or indeed the possibility of not finding a panda. Instead, most choose a panda sanctuary where a meeting is guaranteed. Dedicated to giant panda conservation, Chengdu Panda Reserve might feel like a panda theme park, but it's an important research and conservation centre, and because it has a captive breeding programme, there may also be the

In the wild, panda mothers will sometimes leave their cubs for two days or longer while they go foraging for food.

chance of seeing newborn cubs. Less than 150km from Chengdu, another sanctuary – the Bifengxia Panda Reserve – sprawls over 60km². Home to 40 giant pandas, it too affords plenty of close-up views.

GIANT PANDA CONSERVATION

China doesn't have the best reputation for protecting wildlife, but it genuinely treasures the giant panda. Ecotourism brings much-needed income to rural communities near panda territory by creating jobs such as nature guides, and encouraging homestay programmes. And although the giant panda tops the bill, a vast array of other fauna and flora is protected by default, too.

The Qinling Mountains in China's Shaanxi Province harbour two panda reserves within some of the country's best remaining high-altitude forests: Foping and Changqing Nature Reserves. Both were established in the late 1990s to protect the habitat of the giant panda, and Foping today boasts an averages of one panda to every 2.5km² – nearly four times the average in China. Both were established in the late 1990s to protect the habitat of the giant panda, and Foping today boasts an average of two pandas per every square kilometre in places – nearly four times the average in China. The World Wildlife Fund has worked closely with the Chinese government to protect habitat and create green corridors, whilst other threats such as poaching and illegal logging have been significantly reduced in recent years

NOT JUST BLACK & WHITE

Giant pandas share their habitat with a distant relative – the red panda. Slightly bigger than a domestic cat, it looks like a cross between a fox and a racoon, with a thick, lush tail that it wraps around itself to keep snug in these chilly mountain climes. Although more widespread than the giant panda, red pandas are even less visible as they spend most of their lives high up in the trees. But looking up, you may also spot Chinese flying squirrels as they make their impressive glides from tree to tree.

▲ Although distantly related to the giant panda, red pandas are more closely allied with racoons and weasels.
▶▶ Giant pandas need to eat up to 20kg of bamboo every day.

DESIGN FLAWS

Giant pandas don't make it easy on themselves. Female pandas choose a solitary life and are fertile for only a few days each year. Reproduction is slow and infant mortality is high, partly because the mother may sometimes accidentally squash her newborn cub. Then their chosen diet – bamboo – is hardly the most nutritious food, forcing them to spend half their lives just eating. But their digestive system, built like that of a carnivore, doesn't cope well, and processes only about 20% of this vegetarian onslaught. If that wasn't enough to hinder them, bamboo also contains a chemical that causes drowsiness; so after feasting, the giant panda needs lengthy periods of sleep. When a male gets a whiff of a female in season he needs to find her as quickly as he can – constantly handicapped by his need to eat and then pass out.

RULE OF THUMB UP

A giant panda has five fingers and one thumb, which comes in handy for stripping leaves off bamboo. This thumb is an extended part of the panda's wrist bone and is cited as classic evidence for evolution. Without it, a giant panda wouldn't have an opposable digit, making it difficult to eat its favourite food. Most other bears are omnivores, eating both meat and vegetation, and all lack this extra thumb. Yet the red panda, which isn't a bear and is more closely related to racoons and skunks, shares this added feature. The discovery of the bones of a previously unknown red panda relative on a Spanish site showed that it too had a false thumb. From fossil evidence, scientists have concluded that this ancient red panda ate some meat. Thus the conclusion is that whereas the giant panda probably evolved its extra digit for eating bamboo, the red panda developed this feature as an aid for locomotion through the forest canopy.

IN BRIEF

SIZE
1.6–1.9m/75–135kg

STATUS
Endangered

HOW
Trekking; panda sanctuary

WHO
Trekking 16+; no age restriction for panda sanctuaries

WHEN
Feb–Apr & Nov

WHERE
CHINA
Wild encounters
- Changqing Nature Reserve
- Fengtongzhai Reserve
- Foping Nature Reserve
- Tangjiahe River Nature Reserve

Panda sanctuaries
- Bifengxia
- Chengdu

TOURS
www.chinagiantpanda.com
www.ecotours.com
www.steppesdiscovery.co.uk
www.wildlifeworldwide.com

FIND OUT MORE
www.pandasinternational.org
www.wildgiantpanda.com
www.worldwildlife.org

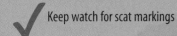 Keep watch for scat markings

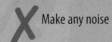 Make any noise

CLIMBING & HIKING IN SEARCH OF
CONDORS & VULTURES

It's early morning at Peru's Colca Canyon, **rays of sunlight** *slanting into* **the void** *below. A hum of* **expectation** *arises from the 30 or so people gathered at the viewing point – like a theatre audience waiting for the curtain to rise. But there's no big entrance, just* **a distant shadow** *down below,* **circling** *gradually higher. Then, out of nowhere, another appears from beneath the rocky lip. Swooping up and over,* **obscuring the sun** *on every revolution, it's so close that I can hear the wind rushing through its wing feathers; see two* **intense** *eyes scanning its domain. Up and up it rises, soaring in* **hypnotic arcs** *until it's gained sufficient height; then it peels off along the valley until it's just a spot against the deep blue sky.*

IAN WOOD

Andean condors climb on morning thermals over Peru's impressive Colca Canyon.

THE ENCOUNTERS

CONDORS

Even if you've a head for heights, staring down into the abyss of Colca Canyon induces a sense of vertigo. Twice the depth of America's Grand Canyon, its vertical walls plummet over 3,200m to the valley floor. Although this area is riddled with trekking possibilities, there is also good road access to El Cruz Condor, a viewing point perched on the edge of the ravine. Small crowds gather here in the early morning, waiting for Andean condors to leave their nests and steadily rise on the thermal currents. With a wingspan that may exceed three metres, these imposing birds specialise in gliding. The edges of their feathered wings look like giant fingertips which they use to make fine adjustments to their flight path, ever on watch for the carcasses on which they feed. On a good day you'll see several Andean condors performing fly-bys along the valley and soaring directly overhead. Further north, similar antics are performed by their endangered North American cousins – California condors.

BEARDED & GRIFFON VULTURES

There is nothing quite like being above a soaring bird of prey to get that thrilling sense of having truly scaled the heights. The Spanish Pyrenees is Europe's raptor central, and hiking the mountain trails of Ordesa

A young Andean condor (above left) does not acquire the adult's red head and white neck ruff until it is six years old.
Bearded vultures, or lammergeiers, are one of the rarest raptors in Europe.

National Park guarantees close encounters. Eurasian griffon vultures are the most conspicuous. Keep a low profile as you approach a ridge top or ravine, and you can peer down on these huge birds sweeping past the ledges below, primaries splayed as they negotiate the updrafts. Others to look out for include smaller Egyptian vultures, aerobatic red kites and – if you're lucky – a golden eagle cruising the ridges. But greatest prize is the bearded vulture, or lammergeier. Known locally as *quebrantahuesos* – 'breaker of bones' – this huge, rare bird is famed for its habit of dropping pieces of carcass from on high to smash into more manageable chunks on the rocks below. Tuck yourself in below the skyline and wait: sooner or later one will glide past, sunlight catching the slate grey of its angled, 2.5m wingspan as it combs the valley for any sign of carrion. Stay still, and curiosity may bring the bird close enough for you to see its glinting eye and moustachioed face.

Roosting on precipitous cliffs in South Africa's Drakensberg Mountains, Cape griffon vultures also leave their nests to soar on morning thermals, often flying over great distances in search of food. Gregarious by nature, you'll hear them cackling and squealing near their roosts or squabbling over carrion. Adults have a creamy plumage trimmed with darker wingtips, and with bare-faced bluish skin around the face and neck. Bearded vultures can be seen here too.

IN BRIEF

SIZE
Andean condor wingspan 3m or more/15kg
Bearded vulture wingspan to 2.7m/7kg
California condor wingspan 3m or more/15kg
Cape griffon vulture wingspan to 1m/9.4kg
Griffon vulture wingspan to 2.7m/12kg

STATUS
Andean condor: near threatened
Bearded vulture & griffon vulture: least concern
California condor: critically endangered
Cape Griffon vulture: vulnerable

HOW
Trekking, climbing

WHO
16+

WHEN & WHERE
1 PERU
• Colca Canyon (all year)

2 SOUTH AFRICA
• Drakensberg Mountains (all year)

3 SPAIN
• Añisclo Canyon, Ordesa National Park (Feb–Sep)
• El Chorro Gorge, Andalucia (all year)

4 USA
• Big Sur, California (all year)

TOURS
www.escapedtoperu.com
www.hikepyrenees.co.uk
www.wildsideholidays.com

FIND OUT MORE
www.peregrinefund.org
www.vulture-territory.com

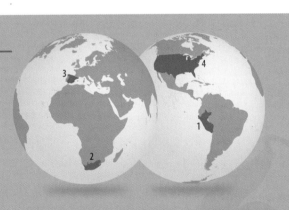

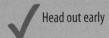 Head out early

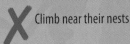 Climb near their nests

POLAR BEAR
ENCOUNTERS

"Y*ou would think that finding a polar bear in the* **Arctic wilderness** *would be fairly difficult but it's not long before we've got word of a sighting.* **Six hundred kilogrammes** *of furry white bear is hard enough to spot with binoculars, but getting close is the real challenge. So our intrepid icebreaker grinds to a halt and we wait. Our* **patience is rewarded** *as the bear eventually starts to make its way over to check out these unexpected visitors. We are kept* **entertained** *for some 30 minutes as the bear plays around, sniffing the ship's bow, jumping between ice floes and* **curiously** *looking up at us hanging over the railings, before he plods off across the ice. Safe on board, we* **keep watch** *until he is out of sight.*"

RENEE SHORTER
www.discover-the-world.co.uk

DISCOVER
THE WORLD

THE ENCOUNTER

POLAR BEARS IN SUMMER

Canada's Hudson Bay offers a rare opportunity to track polar bears on foot without having to gear up for snow and ice. From June onwards, the bears gather around the western shoreline, waiting for the November freeze, when they will head out in search of seals. They are generally easy to find, being conspicuous against the treeless, summer terrain and leaving their five-toed tracks printed on any exposed ground. Nonetheless, an individual can pop up suddenly from behind a low thicket or one of the glacial boulders scattered across the bay at low tide, so – as with bears anywhere – supreme caution is necessary. Your guides will carry an arsenal of deterrents, from firecracker and pepper spray to loaded shotgun, but these are for emergency only. Experience has taught them how to read a bear's behaviour and direct the group accordingly, allowing you to get close enough for a good view without causing the animal any undue stress. A relaxed individual that has encountered humans before may allow you to approach within a pulse-quickening 40m. If it becomes too curious for comfort, your guide's lusty yells and well-aimed stones will help change its mind.

▲   With a backdrop of tundra alive with flora and fauna, polar bears can be seen in summertime too.
◀◀   Polar bears have an acute sense of smell and are capable of sniffing out prey several kilometres away.

TUNDRA BUGGY

On the shore of Hudson Bay, the town of Churchill bills itself as the polar bear capital of the world. During October and November, polar bears move out onto newly formed ice in search of seals and this area becomes a magnet for polar bear tourism. Purpose-built 'tundra buggies' – like Portakabins on wheels – trundle across the snowy terrain providing a safe and comfortable option for extremely close-up views of polar bears and other wildlife. It's not uncommon for bears to come right up and peer in the windows, and some vehicles also have outside decks for open-air viewing.

ARCTIC ADVENTURES

Nestled half way between mainland Norway and the North Pole, the Svalbard archipelago has more polar bears than people. Add in the perpetual summer daylight and you'll see why the region offers some of the best chances to see this iconic animal. Several ships visit Svalbard, sometimes eerily forging through mist and ice, at others cruising under clear blue skies. Polar bears are usually seen at close quarters from the safety of the bridge, bow and decks, with Zodiac boats providing further opportunities for more eye-level sightings, and some time spent ashore each day.

▲   Polar bear habitat is shrinking due to global warming.

▶▶   Walrus herds have clearly defined social structures based on tusk size, body size and aggressiveness.

I AM THE WALRUS

Despite the polar bear's impressive size it does not live completely free from danger. Occasionally, wolves can try to separate a mother from her young, but the only animal that they have reason to fear — apart from man — is the walrus. Powerful and aggressive, these ivory-tusked beasts can be a match for the polar bear and occasionally the two combatants have been known to fight to the death.

ARCTIC FOX

Arctic foxes share this tundra, sometimes scavenging on the remains of food that polar bears have left behind. With smaller, more rounded ears than a red fox, they have the warmest fur of any mammal — thick and lush to protect them from the bitter cold. Their furry feet pads are also designed for life in the Arctic; not only providing a layer of insulation but also giving extra traction on the ice.

POLAR BEAR SAFETY

The death of Horatio Chapple in August 2011 tragically reinforced that polar bears can be extremely dangerous. Part of a group from the British Schools Exploring Society, Horatio was killed when a polar bear attacked his campsite in Svalbard. Safety procedures had not been observed.

On average, three polar bears are killed each year in this region due to humans taking defensive action when trekking or camping. The Norwegian Polar Institute (www.npolar.no) has issued guidelines to reduce the risk of confrontations. Most important is to ensure that you are with a guide who understands the importance of carrying a flare gun and a high-powered rifle – and knows how and when to use them. Should you spot a bear at a distance, avoid conflict by staying out of its path; never move towards it. If a bear moves towards you, you can still avert trouble by shouting and clapping, and starting the engine of a snow mobile. If this fails, it's time for the flare gun, aiming so that the flare lands between your group and the bear, not behind it. As an absolute last resort – if an aggressive bear attacks with no sign of being scared away – the advice is to shoot to kill. The overriding question is whether this kind of tourism is an acceptable risk – for bears as well as humans.

IN BRIEF

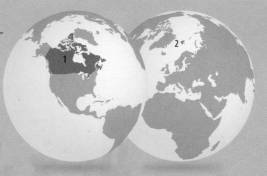

SIZE
Up to 2.8m/800kg

STATUS
Vulnerable

HOW
Boat, foot & tundra buggy

WHO
Foot 18+; boat & tundra buggy 12+

WHEN & WHERE
1 CANADA
• Hudson Bay: summer tundra Jun–Sep; tundra buggy Oct–Nov
• Nunavut (Jul–Nov)

2 NORWAY
Svalbard (Jun–Sep)

TOURS
www.discover-the-world.co.uk (see page 179)
www.exodus.co.uk
www.frontiersnorth.com
www.worldbearsafaris.com

FIND OUT MORE
www.polarbearsalive.org
www.polarbearsinternational.org

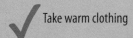 Take warm clothing

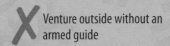 Venture outside without an armed guide

PENGUINS
KAYAKING, WALKING & CAMPING

" *The iceberg **glows an iridescent blue**, as if lit from within. Kayaking through this silent world, I'm overwhelmed by the sheer **scale of beauty**. A wall of white dominates the landscape, rising from the ice sheet, backlit by **a neon sky**. In single file, a group of Adélie penguins waddles towards the ocean, **comical yet elegant**. Reaching a slope they launch forward on their bellies, tobogganing down towards the water. At the shoreline, they resume an upright posture, shuffling on their feet. Then, one by one, they dive into the icy water – darting like **individual torpedoes** beneath my boat.* "

LIZ LUNNON
www.discover-the-world.co.uk

DISCOVER
THE WORLD

ANTARCTIC ENCOUNTERS

As your ship lurches through rolling seas, you'll have plenty of time to contemplate what lies ahead. But the truth is – nothing can prepare you for Antarctica. Our coldest, driest, windiest continent is surrounded by nutrient-rich waters but has no permanent human population. Thus, unfazed by your presence, the wildlife goes about its everyday life.

Your mother ship might be the base, but there are several ways to observe penguins much nearer. Set foot on Antarctica and you should try to keep at least five metres away from penguins, but in practice this is quite a feat. Many have no fear of humans and the more curious ones will shamble up to you, trying to peck you gently on the leg. Kayak with a guide along the shoreline for a close-up view of giant penguin rookeries: busy raucous gatherings with an over-whelming stench of rotting fish. The duration of your kayak trip will vary according to your comfort level, but many are suitable for novices. Or for perhaps the ultimate encounter, trek across the wilderness and camp overnight near an emperor penguin colony.

FLYING FISH?

Penguin colonies can vary from just a few breeding pairs to over half-a-million birds — busy, raucous gatherings with an overwhelming stench of rotting fish. Indeed, early Antarctic explorers classified penguins as fish — and when you see them flying through the water you'll understand their thinking. Perfect hydrodynamic bodies and bulging paddle muscles help propel them at speeds of up to 40km. On land, though, they're not so elegant, a situation that would be comic if it didn't make them so vulnerable to predators such as sea lions.

▲ Penguin rookeries can number thousands of individuals, who go about their lives unfazed by human visitors.
◀◀ Adélie penguins gather at the edge of the sea before diving in for a fishing trip.

SUMMER BONUS

Summer brings millions of migrant birds to the Antarctic, including both Arctic and Antarctic terns. Gregarious by nature, they fish in large flocks, diving into the ocean to snag fish. Antarctic terns migrate each winter to feed in warmer South African waters, but this is nothing compared with the epic journey undertaken by their Arctic namesakes. Leaving Greenland in late August, they fly over 15,000km, arriving in Antarctica for summer before setting off back home.

You're also likely to come surprisingly close to some of the eight species of whale that migrate to Antarctic waters. Of these, Minke whales will often approach a ship, crossing the bows and sometimes surfacing just metres away. You may spot leopard seals, too, waiting by icy ledges to pounce on penguins as they dive into the water.

ANTARCTIC TOURISM

Nearly 40,000 tourists visit Antarctica annually, causing concern that such numbers will both damage the marine environment and interfere with research programmes. The International Association of Antarctica Tour Operators (www.iaato.org) aims to ensure that tourism is carried out with respect for both the wildlife and the environment. At all times, but especially in the breeding season, it is important not to disturb any wildlife or approach animals in a way that could cause them to alter their behaviour.

▲   Penguins are the favourite food for leopard seals, making up almost 90% of their diet.
▶▶ Mother emperor penguins take care of their chicks using the warmth of their brood pouches.

WARMER CLIMES

Antarctica may be synonymous with penguins but they also live elsewhere. African penguins mostly inhabit inshore islands from Namibia to South Africa, but the colony in South Africa's Boulders Bay has become famous. Numbering over 2,500, they have virtually no fear of humans, stepping on your beach towel and darting around you when you're in the water. Australia and New Zealand are home to other species such as the blue penguin, while the Galápagos boasts the only Equatorial penguins on the planet.

PATERNAL DUTIES

There is only one bird that breeds in the perpetual darkness of an Antarctic winter – the regal emperor penguin. Between April and September, temperatures can plummet below −50°C and wind speeds have been recorded in excess of 170km/h, yet during May the female lays a single egg. Not that she's involved in the incubation process. The egg is carefully passed over to balance on her partner's feet, and for the next nine weeks it will be his sole responsibility. While she heads off across the ice in search of the open ocean and a feast of fish, he will eat no food, losing about a third of his body weight. Huddling together for warmth, the males endure the bitter winter, waiting for the chicks to hatch and their females to return.

IN BRIEF

SIZE
From little blue, 30cm/1.5kg; to emperor, 1.1m/40kg

STATUS
African, Galápagos, northern rockhopper, yellow-eyed, all endangered

HOW
Boat, kayak & on foot

WHO
Some ships have minimum age limits from 6 to 12+

WHEN & WHERE
1 ANTARCTICA & THE SUB-ANTARCTIC ISLANDS
Adélie, emperor, chinstrap, gentoo, king, rockhopper, Magellanic & macaroni penguins (Nov–Mar)
www.antarcticabound.com, www.falklandstravel.com, www.wildlifeadventures.com

2 ARGENTINA
• Isla Martillo
Gentoo & Magellanic penguins (Sep–Apr)
www.piratour.com.ar

3 AUSTRALIA
• Penguin & Phillip Islands
Little (blue) penguins (Sep–Jun)
www.penguinisland.com.au, www.penguins.org.au

4 ECUADOR
• Galápagos Islands
Galápagos penguins (all year)
www.southernexplorations.com

5 NEW ZEALAND
• South Island (southeast) & Stewart Island
Fiordland, blue & yellow-eye penguins (Sep–Jun)
www.stewart-island.nz.com

6 SOUTH AFRICA
• Boulders Bay
African penguins (all year)

TOURS
www.discover-the-world.co.uk (see page 179)
www.exodus.co.uk

FIND OUT MORE
www.penguins-world.com

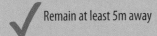 Remain at least 5m away   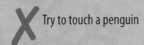 Try to touch a penguin

WATCHING
HIPPOS

"Wallowing in the sun, the hippos look like **giant boulders**, sleeping close together, rows of nostrils just above the water. There's the occasional **twitch of an ear** and then a **clumsy** movement, as a hippo shifts its body, trying to get more comfortable. This triggers a chain reaction, as others move and groan. One seems particularly irritable about his wake-up call. Standing, its mouth opens, tusks and teeth **glisten in the sun**; like a giant bucket, it scoops up water and **hurls it** on its neighbour. But this just causes more **upheaval**; grunts and gripes **ripple through the herd**, each hippo jostling for prime position before **sloshing** back down in the mud."

IAN WOOD

THE ENCOUNTER

Game-viewing boats afford a safe way to see hippos at close quarters, but in many places you can also set out by canoe. You'll need an experienced guide though – get too close and you run a serious risk of attack. Hides are another option; located right next to watering holes, they sometimes allow night-time viewing to watch the hippos feed. But Mzima Springs in Tsavo West National Park, Kenya, adds a whole new dimension – an underwater hide where you'll see hippos moonwalk across the muddy floor.

A FEARSOME FOE

'Fat and bald' may conjure up the image of a harmless creature, but hippos are aggressive. People in the know consider them among the most dangerous beasts in Africa – not including humans and mosquitoes. Never get between a hippo and the water, or a mother and its calf, or you risk meeting it head on in a fearsome charge. Despite weighing more than a car, hippos can run surprisingly fast – bellowing and swinging their gaping mouths like a giant-toothed sledgehammer.

▲   Exercise caution when watching hippos and never get between them and the water.

◀◀ A bloat of hippos can number in excess of 30 individuals.

PYGMY HIPPOS

Substantially smaller than the common hippo, these elusive animals are now restricted to a small area of west Africa. Tai National Park in Ivory Coast is their last stronghold, but you'll need luck and determination even to catch a glimpse – these hippos are solitary, nocturnal and prefer dense forest habitat.

CLEANED FROM TOP TO TAIL

Plenty of birds share the waters where hippos like to wallow, but oxpeckers go one stage further, perching on their bodies and pecking at the skin. It's a symbiotic relationship, this: the hippos get rid of unwanted parasites and the birds get an easy meal. Both species – red-billed and yellow-billed – are about the size of a starling, with short legs and sharp claws enabling them to cling on at precarious angles. But whether it's a completely equal deal is open to debate as they also peck at cuts, delaying the healing process and attracting more parasites.

IN BRIEF

SIZE
Common hippo 2.7m/1,400kg;
pygmy hippo 1.5m/270kg

STATUS
Common hippo vulnerable; pygmy hippo endangered

HOW
Hide, boat & foot

WHO
No age limit

WHEN & WHERE

1 BOTSWANA
• Okavango Delta (all year)
• Chobe National Park (all year)

2 GHANA
• Wechiau Community Hippo Sanctuary (Nov–Jun)
  www.ghanahippos.com

3 IVORY COAST
• Tai National Park (all year)

4 KENYA
• Mzima Springs, Tsavo West National Park (Jan, Feb & Jun–Sep)

5 MALAWI
• Mvuu Camp, Liwonde National Park (Apr–Nov)

6 SOUTH AFRICA
• Shapandani Hide, Kruger National Park (all year)
• Pilanesberg Game Reserve (all year)

7 TANZANIA
• The Retreat, Selous Game Reserve (Jun–Nov)

8 UGANDA
• Kazinga Channel, Queen Elizabeth National Park (all year)

9 ZAMBIA
• Kaingo Camp, South Luangwa National Park (May–Oct)
• Lower Zambezi National Park (Jun–Oct)

10 ZIMBABWE
• Mana Pools National Park (May–Oct)

TOURS
www.expertafrica.com
www.steppestravel.co.uk
www.wildlifeworldwide.com

FIND OUT MORE
www.hippoworlds.com

 Remember that hippos are dangerous   Get between a hippo and the water

KAYAKING WITH
ALLIGATORS
IN THE EVERGLADES

"The sky is misted by **wispy clouds**, perfectly mirrored in the glassy water. As I paddle through tunnels of twisted mangroves, the tip of my kayak sends **ripples** out towards the gnarled edges. There's a sudden splash and an eagle rises from the spray, clutching a fish in its talons. Drifting further, I spot **two eyes** and **a pair of nostrils** floating just above the creek. Nearer now; I can see its scaly body beneath the surface: a three-metre-long **alligator**, watching me, **unblinking**. As I move to steer away, it sinks, slowly, leaving a trail of rising bubbles and mini whirlpools. Protected by just a thin layer of plastic, I raise my oars, **hold my breath** and glide on through."

IAN WOOD

Alligators have a varied diet including crabs, frogs, turtles, snakes, wading birds, otters, deer and even other alligators.

THE ENCOUNTER

Kayaking through the Everglades is a world apart from the noisy airboats of most Florida waterways. No chugging engine; just the sounds of nature and the gentle splashing of oars. Even the wildlife ignores you, seeing the vessel, not the feared human face.

As you set out along narrow backwaters, or lakes of sawgrass spreading out towards the horizon, there will be plenty of opportunities to observe alligators sunbathing along the bank or floating, motionless, in the water.

Guided trips will enhance your experience, but this is a safe area for a competent kayaker to explore alone. Alligators won't attack or try to roll a kayak and will usually leave as you approach, but always respect their personal space and try to keep at least three metres away.

CROCODILES TOO

The Everglades is the only place in the world where alligators and crocodiles co-exist – the latter confined to the brackish waters of Florida Bay. At first glance it's hard to tell them apart, but look at the colour of their skin and the shape of their mouths. Crocodiles have a lighter, greyish complexion and a much narrower, triangular-shaped snout compared with that of the broader alligator.

Kayaking quietly allows you to get closer to the alligators and crocodiles of the Everglades.
With luck you could also see a manatee whilst kayaking in the Everglades.

WADING BIRDS & MANATEES

The Everglades' champagne-coloured waters are home to a profusion of over 300 bird species. The white ibis forages in dense colonies, sometimes numbering several thousand. On orange legs, they wade through the shallow waters, slender bills sweeping side to side as they probe the mud in search of crayfish. The rarer wood stork has a more unusual method of fishing: immersing its large black beak, it stirs the water with its feet. Fish are dazed in the confusion – allowing the storks to pluck them out with ease. Down below, manatees, or sea cows, feed lazily on beds of coastal seagrass, rising to the surface to exhale a spray of mist before refilling their lungs, and making the occasional foray to inland creeks for fresh water.

SHRINKING SWAMP

Over the last century, the Everglades has shrunk by half, a victim of both urban sprawl and the needs of the farming industry. Water for these is diverted both to and away from lakes and rivers, disturbing the delicate balance of this ecosystem. Invasive species are the other threat, in the form of melaleuca trees. Native to Australia, they grow in both terrestrial and aquatic habitats and have now taken over large areas of the Everglades, creating an environment that is alien to native plants and animals. Fortunately, help is at hand in the form of the Everglades Coalition, an alliance of more than 50 conservation and environmental organisations that is dedicated to both protecting and restoring these important wetlands.

IN BRIEF

SIZE
American alligator up to 4.6m/450kg
American crocodile up to 4.6m/900kg

STATUS
American alligator, least concern
American crocodile, vulnerable

HOW
Kayak

WHO
No age limit but children need to be
accompanied by an adult.

WHEN
All year

WHERE
USA
• Everglades National Park

TOURS
www.evergladesadventures.com
www.evergladesareatours.com
www.kayakfloridakeys.com

FIND OUT MORE
www.everglades.national-park.com
www.evergladescoalition.org

 Take a hat

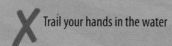 Trail your hands in the water

THE PANTANAL
JAGUARS & MORE

> *It takes a lot of hard staring before your eyes decipher the pattern of spots among the* **dappled tangle**. *But suddenly the image resolves, like one of those 'Magic Eye' picture puzzles, and there it is:* **a jaguar**, *lying on the riverbank in full view. Your guide kills the motor and* **nudges** *you forward with his paddle. You* **drift** *to a halt among a knot of floating roots just ten metres from those* **piercing** *amber eyes.* **One bound** *away.*

MIKE UNWIN

Jaguars range widely across Latin America, from the Mexican rainforest to the Argentinian pampas. But so mythically elusive are these big cats that few wildlife destinations dare advertise their presence as a visitor attraction. Few, that is, apart from the Pantanal. This vast wetland, which sprawls across some 200,000km² of Brazil and over into Paraguay and Bolivia, has a growing reputation for close encounters with the continent's largest predator.

Your best chance of meeting one is by water. During the dry season, when the floods recede, wildlife concentrates by permanent pools and rivers – and it is along the larger rivers that the big cats are most reliably seen, roaming the banks in search of prey and seeking out the cooling river breezes for their siesta. Local guides – some descended from jaguar-hunting Pantaneiro stock – know exactly where to look for them.

But it's not all jaguars. River trips bring a pageant of other wildlife, including countless yacare caimans cruising the shallows; prehistoric-looking green iguanas draped across overhanging branches; grazing family groups of sheep-sized, semi-aquatic capybaras (the world's largest rodent); and, if you're lucky, a South American tapir cooling its bulk in a blackwater

creek. Along larger rivers, such as the Cuiaba or Pixaim, you might also encounter a pack of giant river otters. These charismatic, endangered predators – known in South America as *lobos del río* (river wolves) – often approach boats, cavorting around the bows and popping up with their struggling catches.

Back on dry land, walking trails allow you to track down some of the Pantanal's forest-dwellers. A rustle in the canopy often betrays the presence of howler or capuchin monkeys, while the leaf-litter at your feet may reveal the diggings of armadillos, a procession of leaf-cutter ants or a shy foraging agouti. Follow boardwalks over the flooded wetlands to get to grips with the prolific birdlife, from egrets, spoonbills and sunbitterns wading through the waterweed to huge-billed toco toucans lurching overhead. And climb the raised viewing platforms for eye-level sightings of nesting jabiru storks, or sweeping savanna vistas that might just include the shaggy silhouette of a wandering giant anteater.

Numerous *fazendas* (ranches) are now geared up for ecotourism. If you can't rouse yourself from your hammock, these properties crawl with wildlife: caimans in the ditches, capybaras cropping the lawns and raucous hyacinth macaws - enormous blue parrots that are the avian stars of the Pantanal - screeching from the tree tops. After dark, spotlighting along local roads allows you to seek out such nocturnal residents as pygmy owls and crab-eating foxes. Your guide's beam will pick out the red eyes of caimans and you might meet an ocelot slinking along the road – or even a jaguar.

Each area of the Pantanal has its highlights: the Cuiaba River region, at the end of the Trans-pantaneira Highway, offers the most reliable jaguar sightings, while the more open grasslands of the southern section offer a better chance of giant anteaters and even the occasional puma. You will need to decide on your priorities and take local advice. Wherever you choose to go, however, this vast wetland remains indisputably South America's best location for sheer variety of wildlife viewing – and your best shot at its top cat.

WHEN Jaguars: all year; best Jul–Sep (end of dry season)
TOURS www.naturetrek.co.uk, www.wildlifetrails.co.uk

As well as jaguars, the Pantanal is home to a wealth of other wildlife, including giant anteaters and vividly coloured birds such as the chestnut-eared araçari.
River journeys offer the best chance of seeing the Pantanal's most prolific wildlife, including yacare caimans and hyacinth macaws.

IN SEARCH OF THE ELUSIVE
SHOEBILL

"*It's almost claustrophobic, paddling a dugout canoe through this swamp, **hemmed in** on either side by tall grasses. Further on, it opens out to a vast area of papyrus as the sun casts hues of red and gold across the sky.*

*I'll **never forget** my first shoebill sighting. Towering above the reeds, unlike any bird I've ever seen, it stands, **frozen in time**, like a giant stuffed animal in a museum. In fact, with bulbous bill and **striking stare**, it bears more than a passing resemblance to a dodo. As we edge closer, just the **ripple of our oars** breaks the silence. Then, for long minutes, there's no movement at all – we, motionless in our canoe; our prey **statuesque**, until its **prehistoric beak** opens with a gaping yawn.*"

IAN WOOD

◀ Shoebills boast the largest bill of all the world's bird species.

THE ENCOUNTER

Shoebills are high up on many birders' must-see lists, but the whole experience of searching for these elusive birds is special in itself. Canoeing slowly through these swamps, clouds of insects buzzing, birds wading and soaring overhead is, quite simply, serene.

Shoebills aren't particularly nervous, so once you've found one – and as long as you approach with care – you should be able to observe it for a while. But they are rare, so local knowledge is essential to find where and when they have been recently sighted. Although they spend great portions of their day just standing still, occasionally they wade slowly through the murky swamps, their oversized bills submerged for long periods of time. Either way, you'll almost certainly need a canoe for this encounter, enabling you to explore the channels of the shoebill's marshy home. The exception is during the dry season in Zambia's Bangweulu Wetlands (May–December), where you can walk over the papyrus reeds for a closer view. And don't think you need to be a passionate birder to take pleasure out of watching a shoebill; without a doubt it will be one of the most extraordinary creatures that you will ever see.

TO GO OR NOT TO GO

Many of the shoebill's wetland habitats are threatened by human activities such as drainage schemes. They are also hunted both for their meat and in order to supply zoos with specimens. Tourism, however,

▲   An impressive wingspan of over two metres is needed to support the shoebill's bulky undercarriage.

can offer alternatives sources of income to local people, and incentives to conserve these areas. In one recent initiative, Zambia's Bangweulu Wetlands have been incorporated within a community partnership park, a new concept designed to rehabilitate the area and protect it for both wildlife and the community.

A NOSE FOR THE UNUSUAL

You don't get the nickname 'whalehead' without good reason – and with one of the largest beaks of any living bird, shoebills deserve it. They certainly make the most of them, too, plunging their beaks in the water to scoop up lungfish and frogs. In the breeding season, males and females engage in elaborate bill-clacking courtships, their foreplay possibly enhanced by their oversized conks. Then, mating over, they use their large bills to scoop up water and pour it over their eggs and chicks to prevent them from overheating in the fierce sun.

IN BRIEF

SIZE
110–150cm/5–7kg

STATUS
Vulnerable

HOW
Canoe & on foot

WHO
No age limit

WHEN
All year

WHERE
1 SUDAN
• Al-Sudd Swamp

2 TANZANIA
• Moyowosi-Kigosi Swamp

3 UGANDA
• Kikorongo Swamp, Queen Elizabeth National Park
• Lake Albert, Semliki Valley Game Reserve
• Mabamba Swamp
• Murchison Falls National Park

4 ZAMBIA
• Bangweulu Wetlands

TOURS
www.expertafrica.com
www.naturetrek.co.uk
www.shoebillsafaris.com

FIND OUT MORE
www.shoebill.com

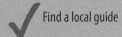 Find a local guide

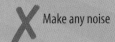 Make any noise

SWIMMING WITH WILD
DOLPHINS

"*The rising sun has opened up **cracks of light** across the ocean. The only sound is the hypnotic chant of our engine as we chug out to sea. Then to the left comes a splash. A dolphin! They're **surfing** in our wake now, **playing**, squeaking. We cut the engine and **I slip overboard** as quietly as possible, surrounded by **whistles** and clicks. Suddenly there they are, **emerging from the blue**: six, no seven, heading **straight towards me**. A mother and calf encircle, clicking, **smiling**, round and round. Another comes so close, turning on its side to get a better look at me. Then it's over and I watch them **fade** back into the deep.*"

AMANDA STAFFORD
www.dolphinconnectionexperience.com (Azores)
www.dolphinswims.co.uk (Egypt, Red Sea)

THE ENCOUNTER

Before you consider swimming with wild dolphins, you need to be a confident swimmer and know how to use a snorkel and mask. Any decent dolphin swim operator will provide you with a thorough briefing beforehand, which should include both on-boat and in-water safety advice. Of course, swimming with wild dolphins is a hit-and-miss affair and can never be guaranteed. Even if you find a pod, you shouldn't enter the water if they are resting or hunting as this can disturb these activities. Wait for the signal from whoever is in charge before you go overboard.

It's vital that you enter the ocean as quietly as possible; if you lunge in with an almighty splash you'll scare the dolphins away. Swim slowly and gracefully, with your arms by your side; then, if the dolphins are interested, they will come to you, and the encounter will be on their terms. (It is pointless chasing after a pod of dolphins as they can swim many times faster than you.) Avoid splashing your fins on the surface, which the dolphins might take as a sign of aggression. But if you have an underwater camera, use it: dolphins love the click when you take a photo and they'll often come right up to the lens to peer inside.

TO GO OR NOT TO GO

The increasing number of people who want to swim with dolphins has caused considerable problems. In places such as Kizimkazi in southern Zanzibar, up to ten fully laden boats head out at the same time in

▲   Swim with your arms by your sides and never chase a dolphin.
◀◀   Bottlenose dolphins are one of the most commonly encountered dolphin species.

search of the one resident pod and it's not uncommon for the captains to compete with each other to drop their group closer. The resulting interference interrupts the dolphins' hunting and resting to such an extent that numbers in these areas have drastically diminished. It's no wonder, then, that the Whale and Dolphin Conservation Society (www.wdcs.org.uk) considers swimming with dolphins 'inappropriate' in most places.

The good news is that there are some ethical projects that have the best interests of the dolphins at their core; if the dolphins are resting or hunting, you won't be able to swim with them. Each trip is led by an expert, with only small groups of people (ideally eight or fewer), and sometimes the participants can help gather data to better understand dolphin conservation.

DOLPHINS IN CAPTIVITY

Never watch or swim with dolphins in captivity. These animals should be free and wild, yet more and more tourist places – often expensive resorts aimed at the family market – boast captive dolphins confined in swimming pools and cordoned-off areas of sea. In order to stock such places, whole pods of dolphins are often rounded up to obtain young females that are then shipped around the world. Many of these die in transit and the rest are often killed for meat. Even places that offer 'dolphin-assisted therapy' (DAT) are now considered to be as bad – and there is no scientific evidence that it works.

Ric O'Barry, the head trainer behind the dolphins used in the 1960s *Flipper* TV series, captured and trained many dolphins at the Miami Seaquarium. Then, in 1969, his favourite dolphin effectively committed suicide in his arms by refusing to breathe. Since then, Ric has dedicated his life to dolphin conservation, winning an Academy Award for Best Documentary in 2010 for his film *The Cove*, about the slaughter of dolphins in Japan.

▲   Hector dolphins are recognised by their rounded dorsal fins.
▸▸ Big-eyed trevally sometimes form huge schools.

ADDED BONUS

Dolphins share their habitat with a huge amount of marine life. They can eat up to 25kg of fish every day so you'll often see shoals of fish such as mackerel and herring. I've also seen turtles, squid and rays while swimming with dolphins and even had the occasional sighting of a whale or shark.

A LOYAL FRIEND

Of the 40 species of dolphin, found in every ocean on the planet, one in particular – the bottlenose dolphin – has consistently befriended man and has even saved lives. In 2007, surfer Todd Endris was attacked three times by a great white shark in Monterey Bay, California, causing serious damage to his leg. As a fellow surfer looked on, six bottlenose dolphins jumped in and out of the water, encircling the stricken surfer and using their flippers to beat the water in agitation. Todd firmly believes that without the dolphins the shark would have killed him: 'They're as smart as humans, and I believe they're capable of empathy. Maybe they were trying to protect their young, or acting on instinct, but they drove the shark away. If they hadn't, there's no doubt in my mind that it would have come back.'

BRAIN BOX

Everyone knows that dolphins are clever, but how clever are they? Like us, dolphins have two different hemispheres to their brains but, unlike us, when they need to sleep they can shut down just one half. In this mode one eye remains spookily open while the other is fast asleep.

Some dolphins have brains significantly larger than our own, and recent research has shown that part of their brain – the part that we associate with intelligence and emotions – has the same convoluted folds as ours. Dolphins sometimes use tools, which indicates complex problem-solving skills, dexterity and intelligence. Scientists have witnessed them killing scorpionfish and using their spiny bodies to coax moray eels out of their lairs. And in Western Australia, they've been spotted using sponges to protect themselves from the barbs of stonefish and stingrays as they forage on the reef.

IN BRIEF

SIZE
Male up to 3m/200kg; female up to 2.5m/160kg

MOST FREQUENTLY ENCOUNTERED
Bottlenose, spinner, common, Atlantic spotted, Hector (New Zealand)

STATUS
Hector dolphins: endangered

HOW
Snorkelling

WHO
Confident swimmers 12–14+, depending on location

WHEN, WHERE & TOURS
1 AUSTRALIA Port Phillip Bay, Melbourne; Rockingham, Western Australia (Oct–Apr) www.dolphins.com.au, www.polperro.co.au

2 AZORES (May–Sep) **www.dolphinconnectionexperience.com** (see page 179)

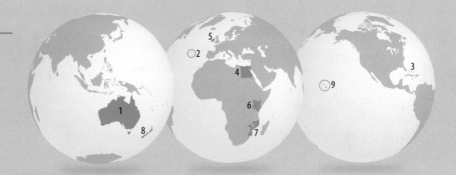

3 BAHAMAS Bimini (May–Aug) www.wilddolphins.com

4 EGYPT Marsa Alam (all year) **www.dophinswims.co.uk** (see page 179)

5 IRELAND Dingle Bay (all year; May–Sep best chance of good weather) www.dingledolphin.com

6 KENYA Kizingo (Nov–Apr) www.kizingo.com

7 MOZAMBIQUE Pemba; Ponto d'Ouro (all year) www.pembadivecamp.com www.somenteaqua.com

8 NEW ZEALAND Bay of Plenty (Oct–Apr) www.swimwithdolphins.co.nz

9 USA Hawaii: Oahu, Kailua (all year) www.dolphinjourneys.com

FIND OUT MORE
www.dolphincareuk.org
www.savejapandolphins.org
www.wdcs.org.uk

 Keep your arms by your side and swim in a calm manner

 Never touch a dolphin

SWIMMING & SNORKELLING WITH
WHALES

"As soon as I'm in the water I can hear their **haunting song** – a deep rumbling sound, not unlike a mooing cow. But then it changes: eerie high-pitched wails, bird-like chirps, blasts and shrieks. A **shiver of anticipation** ripples across my skin as my first humpback whale **looms** out of the clear blue water: swimming on his back, pectoral fins pointing up to the light. Then, **breaking the surface**, he sweeps back down and heads straight towards me, passing within barely ten metres. I feel no sense of trepidation; just **pure unadulterated awe**. His giant lower lip makes him look as if he's smiling and inside my mask I find myself **smiling** back. "

IAN WOOD

◄ Humpback whales have been documented making the longest known migration journey of any mammal species.

THE ENCOUNTERS

SWIMMING WITH HUMPBACK WHALES

Sharing the ocean with humpback whales is a privilege. Imagine slipping into the water, far from land, knowing that humpback whales are close by. Sometimes their appearance will be fleeting – just a few seconds – but even that's enough. At other times they can be extremely curious, and in places such as Tonga in the South Pacific you may well observe mothers with their calves.

It's essential that you choose a fully licensed operator who follows all the guidelines. Usually, only four people plus a guide are allowed in the water at the same time and you must keep a minimum of five metres away. Open seas can be choppy so you'll need to be fit and have some snorkelling experience.

Once a whale has approached, the interaction can last anything from a few minutes to more than an hour, depending on their curiosity. It's important to let the encounter happen on the whales' terms. Calmly floating together in a small group will maximise the chance that their

LOVE SONG

Australia's east coast humpback whales have changed their tune recently – all in the name of love. The male humpback produces sounds as a way of serenading the opposite sex and their style depends on where they live. In 1996, scientists found that two whales in eastern Australia were singing a completely new song, almost identical to other whales that had visited from the Indian Ocean. Within just a year, numerous humpbacks had switched to the new song as they migrated back down the east coast. Clearly it was a hit with the ladies.

▲ Stay calmly floating on the surface so that any interaction with a humpback happens on the whale's terms.

natural curiosity will draw them nearer. Like this, the whales remain in control of both the distance and the duration of your encounter – leaving you to handle the inevitable rush of adrenalin at that first sighting.

CLOSE UP WITH BELUGAS

More than 25,000 belugas spend July and August in Canada's western Hudson Bay. You can see their white bodies clustered far below as you fly in, or watch them blowing in the shallows just outside the town of Churchill. But for a truly intimate perspective you need to join them in the water. Your guide will motor out by Zodiac to a prime spot where, kitted out in dry suit, mask and snorkel, you will lower yourself into the cold water. There's no need to swim. Instead, a noose is roped around your feet, the line paid out behind the boat, and you are dragged slowly backwards with instructions simply to sing. At first, in the cold and dark, your efforts feel ludicrous. But these vocal cetaceans are intensely curious. Soon, in response to your warbling, you will hear the strange radio static of their underwater communications. And moments later they arrive: first, just ghostly shapes in the murk, but soon swimming right up to eyeball you from point-blank. As you relax, and the whales cavort around you – some in pods of five or six, youngsters piggy-backing on females – you can take in their bulbous foreheads and beaky smiles, and enjoy the extraordinary song of the 'sea canary'.

▲　　With blunt heads, no dorsal fins and distinctive white bodies, belugas are one of the most recognisable species of whale.

▶▶　　Killer whales – or orcas - are toothed whales belonging to the dolphin family.

PREDATORY PROWESS

You don't get the nickname 'killer' without some justification and these whales are fearsome predators. Like a pack of wolves or a pride of lions they'll often hunt together, encircling and herding prey before attacking. Needing to eat over 200kg every day leads to a varied diet with fish, squid, seals, sea lions, walruses, turtles, otters, penguins, reptiles, octopus and sharks all on their menu. The latter could seem a dangerous prospect but killer whales have devised several strategies for tackling sharks, with the most impressive being akin to a karate chop. Using their tails, they create an upthrust which pushes the shark to the surface. The whale then spins round, lifting its fluke out of the water before crashing down and stunning the shark.

SWIMMING WITH KILLER WHALES

In 1987 huge quantities of herring chose Tysfjord in Norway as their new wintering ground, shortly to be followed by hundreds of killer whales, or orcas (which are actually classified as the largest of the dolphin species). Donning a dry suit to protect yourself from the icy water and heading out on a Zodiac boat in search of these apparently fearsome creatures is the ultimate whale-watching thrill. Even the name, 'killer', instils terror to temper the joy. Yet humans aren't their natural prey and, despite their reputation, there hasn't been a single attack on snorkellers. It's killer whales in captivity that pose the real threat, with two dozen attacks on handlers reported since the 1970s.

IN BRIEF

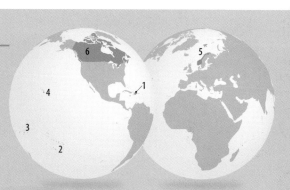

SIZE
Humpback male 13.5m, female 14.5m/both to 45,000kg; killer whale 7–10m/to 5,400kg; beluga to 5m/1,500kg

STATUS
Humpback, least concern (but 2 sub-populations endangered); killer whale, data deficient; beluga, near threatened

HOW
Snorkelling

WHO
16+

WHEN, WHERE & TOURS
Humpback whale
1 DOMINICAN REPUBLIC
• Silver Bank (Jan–Mar) www.aquaticadventures.com

2 FRENCH POLYNESIA
• Rurutu (Jul–Oct) www.diveworldwide.com

3 TONGA
• Vava'u (Jul–Oct) www.whaleswim.com

4 USA
• Kona Coast, Hawaii (Dec–May) www.oceanecotours.com

Killer whale
5 NORWAY
• Tysfjord (Oct–Nov) www.orcasafari.co.uk

Beluga whale
6 CANADA
• Hudson Bay (Jul–Aug) www.seanorthtours.com

FIND OUT MORE
www.wdcs.org
www.whaleresearch.org
www.whaletrust.org

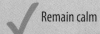 Remain calm

 Duck dive

DIVING WITH
SEALS & SEA LIONS

"As they **shoot past**, a group of grey seals takes a peek, before abruptly turning back. They're like different animals underwater: streamlined; no cumbersome blubber to be seen. One darts in my direction – **bright inquisitive eyes**, whiskers **glinting** in the sun. It's almost up against my mask now, staring in through bulging eyes. I don't feel threatened; this animal **exudes playfulness** from every pore. But, the **sheer speed** of its examination is thrilling; spinning round, it brushes against my wetsuit and I feel it gently nibbling on my fins. Then, **curiosity** satisfied, it streaks away, flippers **gracefully** guiding it through the water in search of its peers. "

IAN WOOD

THE ENCOUNTER

Diving is the best way to see the true agility of seals and sea lions, whose enquiring faces and acrobatic movements make for some of the most stimulating encounters in the marine world. Masters of the water, both can dive deeper than 200m and hold their breath for over half an hour. There's no point in trying to follow them; it's better to wait and trust their inquisitiveness to get the better of them. Often it's the pups that will come closest, peeling away from the group as if being dared by their playmates. If they show interest, you can hold their attention by spinning and rolling around; they'll often stay and play. The bulls patrol their charges from a distance and rarely come too near, but you do need to be aware of them. Avoid diving during the mating season and if a male exhibits territorial behaviour such as barking, get out of the water.

ALL EARS

Many people confuse seals and sea lions. Both have flippers to propel them through the water, layers of blubber to keep them warm, and a liking for fish. If in doubt look at their ears; sea lions have small flaps on either side of their heads, whereas seals just have tiny slits. The exception is the fur seal which, despite its name, does have ears, and is closely related to the sea lion.

▲ Galápagos sea lions can be very inquisitive.
◤ A grey seal having a scratch in the afternoon sun.
◀◀ Thousands of California sea lions inhabit the Channel Islands National Marine Sanctuary, USA.

HOT & COLD

Seals and sea lions rely on thick layers of fatty blubber to aid buoyancy, act as food reserves and reduce heat loss when diving in chilly waters. As mammals, they need to maintain a body temperature of about 37°C, but with such good insulation they can overheat on land. This is why you'll often observe them waving their flippers in the air, as if fanning themselves. In fact, their flippers have large peripheral blood supplies which help to dissipate the extra heat as they waft them through the air.

IN BRIEF

SIZE
Sea lions: from Australian, up to 2.5m/300kg, to Steller, up to 3.3m/900kg
Seals: from Baikal, up to 1.4m/70kg, to elephant, up to 5m/3,000kg

STATUS
Sea lions: Most either endangered or vulnerable. California, South American: least concern; Steller, Australian & Galápagos: endangered; New Zealand: vulnerable.
Seals: 35 species; 7 commonly encountered. Grey, harbour, leopard, Antarctic fur & southern elephant: least concern; Galápagos fur: endangered

HOW
Diving & snorkelling

WHO
Diving 18+

WHEN & WHERE
Seals
1 AUSTRALIA
• Jervis Bay (Jun–Sep)
• Port Phillip Bay (Sep–May)

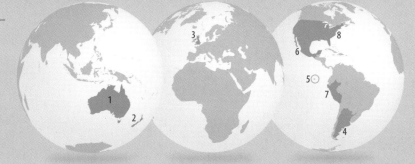

2 NEW ZEALAND
• Marlborough Sounds Marine Park (all year)

3 UK (Jul–Oct)
• Farne Islands (www.farneislanddivers.co.uk)
• Lundy Island
• Western Rocks, Isles of Scilly

Sea lions
4 ARGENTINA
• Punta Loma (Sep–Feb)

5 ECUADOR
• Galápagos Islands (all year)

6 MEXICO
• Cabo san Lucas (all year)

7 PERU
• Islas Palomino, Lima (all year)
  www.nature-expeditions-peru.com

8 USA
• Channel Islands National Marine Sanctuary, California (all year)

TOURS
www.diveworldwide.com
www.oceanwide-expeditions.com

FIND OUT MORE
www.pinnipeds.org
www.seals-world.com

 Wait for them to approach you   Get between a bull and his harem

CLOSE ENCOUNTERS IN
THE GALÁPAGOS

"*Fifty thousand sea lions make their home in the Galápagos, but today **I'm mesmerised** by just this one, practically at my feet. Taking no notice of me or my camera, the pup propels itself slowly up the beach towards its mother **dozing in the sun**, and announces its arrival with a yelp. Rolling over, she **carefully embraces** her offspring with powerful foreflippers until eventually they fall asleep together. It's a scene I will **never forget**.*"

JUSTIN LAYCOB
www.southernexplorations.com

Galápagos sea lions are one of the most conspicuous and numerous of the marine mammals on these islands.

NATURE'S PLAYGROUND

When Charles Darwin first visited the Galápagos Islands in 1835 he was struck not just by the array of wildlife, but also by its fearless nature. Today, while the animals remain unafraid, visitors are restricted to specific areas by the Galápagos National Park authorities. All the same, you'll be rewarded with some of the closest wildlife encounters anywhere on earth. Whether it's trekking on lava trails, roaming along white sandy beaches or hiking to the top of dormant volcanoes – you'll witness animals oblivious to your presence.

⏫ Male blue-footed boobies flaunt their feet and dance to impress a female.
🔺 Marine iguanas and the Galápagos tortoise are just two of many species that are endemic to the islands.
🔻 Male magnificent frigatebirds inflate their throats to impress the ladies.

TROUBLED ISLANDS

In the 1950s about a thousand people lived on the Galápagos and visitors were extremely rare. Today the resident population of some 40,000 is swelled by nearly 200,000 tourists annually and there is serious concern about the effects on the flora and fauna. Protected areas and visitor sites are managed through techniques such as restricting trails, and all visitors must be accompanied by a guide.

A typical day will involve cruising to individual landing sites, which range from 'wet landings' on beaches to 'dry landings' with piers and walkways. Either way, you will usually be greeted by the local residents. Guides often have to shoo away large male sea lions, and concentration is required to avoid stepping on marine iguanas as they sunbathe on the black volcanic rocks. Clicking, screeching albatrosses stare back from close quarters while a plethora of birds such as gulls, terns and pelicans stand their ground. Trails lead through areas where blue-footed boobies go about their mating dance – so near that they'll even make half-hearted pecks at the legs of passing tourists. Longer treks lead into the lush evergreen forests of the highlands for a chance to encounter giant tortoises in the wild. Kayak through these waters and you may well see dolphins, turtles and whales very near your boat. Or take to the water and snorkel or dive among inquisitive sea lions or harmless reef sharks passing through. Specialist dive operators also explore the northern islands of Wolf and Darwin where schooling hammerhead sharks and manta rays abound.

IN BRIEF

HOW
Boat, kayak, snorkel, dive & on foot

WHO
Ship sometimes 6+ or 12+; diving 18+

WHEN
All year unless specified

WAVED ALBATROSS
SIZE Wingspan to 2.4m/4kg
WHERE Española (Apr–Dec)

BLUE-FOOTED BOOBY
SIZE Wingspan to 1.5m/1.5kg
WHERE Common throughout; best colonies on Española & North Seymour

MAGNIFICENT FRIGATEBIRD
SIZE Wingspan to 2.2m/1.8kg
WHERE Genovesa, Seymour & San Cristóbal

MARINE IGUANAS
SIZE Up to 1.5m/1.5kg
WHERE Common along entire coastline

GALÁPAGOS FUR SEAL
SIZE Up to 1.5m/60kg
WHERE Several rocky islets; Genovesa is best

GALÁPAGOS PENGUIN
SIZE Up to 0.5m/2.5kg
WHERE Fernandina, Isabela & Bartolomé

GALÁPAGOS SEA LION
SIZE Up to 2.5m/400kg
WHERE All islands; good snorkelling near Bartolomé, Fernandina, Isabela & Floreana

GALÁPAGOS TORTOISE
SIZE Up to 1.2m/215kg
WHERE Santa Cruz & San Cristóbal

TOURS
www.southernexplorations.com (see page 179)
www.ecoventura.com
www.wildernessjourneys.com

FIND OUT MORE
www.galapagos.org
www.galapagosislands.com

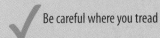 Be careful where you tread

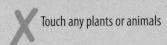 Touch any plants or animals

SNORKELLING ON A
CORAL REEF

"*From the water's edge it looks **idyllic**. Small waves lick the white sand, **softly shifting** underfoot. Turquoise sea, **shimmering** in iridescent light; blue sky brushed by wisps of cloud. As I snorkel out from shore, the sand **gently slopes** away, dappled by specks of **dancing sun**. Over the reef, the water is as **clear** as gin, revealing an **underwater city** beneath my mask with intricate patterns, colours pulsating with the **rhythm of the sea**.*"

IAN WOOD

Schooling bannerfish and clownfish are just a couple of the many species that you're likely to see on a coral reef.

The architects of coral reefs are tiny spine-less animals called polyps, which create a protective skeleton by secreting limestone from their base. When they die, new ones form on top, slowly building these elaborate structures. But polyps can't take the credit for this blaze of colour as their bodies are clear and – like humans – their skeletons are white. It's thanks to algae living in their tissues that they radiate such beauty. Through photosynthesis the algae produces substances that nourish the polyps and in return the algae feeds on the polyps' waste materials. It's a fragile partnership; a slight rise in sea temperature makes the polyps expel the algae, leading to expanses of bleached white coral.

At the base of the reef a spotted goby guards its burrow, while a small yellow shrimp labours, constantly sweeping and clearing sand from near the hole. As I swim nearer, both dart inside the cavity. It's a symbiotic relationship; the goby is the lookout – alert to signs of danger – and in return the shrimp maintains their home.

I'm studying the grooves and patterns of a large boulder of brain coral when a school of bannerfish flutters by. With perfect synchronisation they suddenly change direction; bands of black, white and yellow, long dorsal fins trailing behind.

Nearby, the fleshy tentacles of a sea anemone sway in the gentle current. Two orange clownfish ripple in its fingers, until I'm overhead. Then one swims right up towards my mask. For a small fish, you have to admire its bravery: bolshy, as if it's trying to escort me off the premises.

Twisted brown fingers of staghorn coral branch up, looking like deer antlers reaching for the light. Lurking in its protective structure, the electric colours of a blue-and-yellow angelfish. Further on, I'm surrounded by thousands of miniature glass fish, parting in perfect harmony as I swim through the shoal.

On its far edge, the reef sharply drops away, plummeting into a dark-blue void. Huge fan corals cling to the side of the wall and slightly deeper down two bumphead parrotfish crunch on the coral. Using their bulbous heads and sharp white teeth, they tear off sections, digesting and then excreting sand from out behind. Next time you lie on a powdery white beach, thank these giant herbivores for all their work.

THE BEST OF THE BEST

1 AUSTRALIA Great Barrier Reef (all year)
2 BAHAMAS Bimini Islands (all year)
3 BELIZE Hol Chan Marine Reserve (all year)
4 CAYMAN ISLANDS (all year)
5 ECUADOR Galápagos Islands (all year)
6 EGYPT Mahmya Island (all year)
7 HAWAII Hanauma Bay, Oahu (all year)
8 INDONESIA Raja Ampat (all year)
9 MALDIVES (all year)
10 SEYCHELLES Port Launay Marine National Park (all year)
11 THAILAND Similan & Surin Islands (Dec–Apr)

▶ Healthy corals owe their vivid colour to algae living in their tissues.

SNORKELLING & DIVING WITH
TURTLES

"A leisurely swim from shore, the coral reef **plunges into the depths** and the turquoise water turns a deep, dark blue. To my right, a hawksbill turtle nibbles on a sponge, tearing off small sections with his beak-like mouth. Hunger satisfied, he **propels himself slowly** in my direction, his marbled shell of amber and brown **dappled by the sun**. His face is that of a comic character, but his soulful eyes seem to harbour the **wisdom** of an **ancient sage**. For a while I swim alongside, gently mimicking the rhythm of his flippers with my hands. Then he rises to the surface for a gulp of air, before swimming off into the blue. I watch his **outline fade**, until I'm distracted by a black-tip reef shark passing beneath."

IAN WOOD

Green sea turtles are such an ancient species that they witnessed the evolution of dinosaurs.

THE ENCOUNTER

Turtles spend large portions of their lives resting, feeding or swimming along a reef, which makes them relatively easy to observe, but if you frantically swim after them, they will soon depart; despite appearances, some can swim at over 30km/h.

If you keep about five metres away, it may be possible to swim alongside a turtle, and if you find one munching on the coral you can sometimes get quite close; approach from ahead, rather than taking it by surprise. To observe a resting turtle, stay well back, so as not to disturb it. Despite that, turtles can be inquisitive and will occasionally come within arm's length, but resist any urge to touch their shells. Like a betrayal of trust – nothing is more guaranteed to make a turtle leave.

FOOD FOR THOUGHT

Humans are responsible for endangering turtles. Imagine living on a remote island with a source of eggs that is high in protein, easy to catch in the water and packed with fleshy meat. But tourism can make a difference. The Banyak Islands of west Sumatra are an important nesting site for green turtles and their numbers were in sharp decline. But since 2006, when a project was established to protect their eggs (www.acehturtleconservation.org), local people have been trained to patrol the beaches, homestays have been built for visitors, and the number of turtles is on the increase.

▲   Remain calm and never touch a turtle, and sometimes you'll be rewarded with an intimate encounter.
▼   The odds of a baby turtle making it to adulthood are about a 1,000 to 1.

THE TEARS OF A TURTLE

On a moonlit night, a pregnant female returns to her birthplace, crawling up the sandy beach to lay her eggs above the high-water line. Legend says that she cries from the pain of giving birth, or out of sadness for abandoning her babies to a perilous future. But the explanation for her tears is more mundane — turtles have a gland which helps them both to get rid of excess salt and to remove sand from their eyes. Once the hatchlings emerge, just getting to the sea is hard enough; only a few centimetres long and weighing less than 30 grams, they're easy prey for birds. Even the ocean is no sanctuary; sharks and carnivorous fish like these tasty morsels too. In fact, the odds against them getting to adulthood are tiny: about 1,000:1!

IN BRIEF

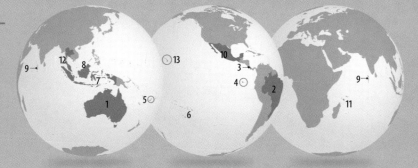

SIZE
From Kemp's ridley, 0.65m/45kg, to leatherback, up to 2m/600kg

STATUS
Leatherback, hawksbill & Kemp's ridley, critically endangered; loggerhead & green, endangered; olive ridley, vulnerable; flatback, data deficient

HOW
Snorkelling & diving

WHO
Diving 18+

WHEN
All year unless specified

WHERE

1 AUSTRALIA
• Bare Sand Island (May–Oct)
• Ribbon Reefs

2 BRAZIL
• Fernando de Noronha

3 COSTA RICA
• Tortuguero National Park

4 ECUADOR
• Galápagos Islands

5 FIJI
• Kadavu Island (Aug–Oct)

6 FRENCH POLYNESIA
• Bora Bora

7 INDONESIA
• Banyak Islands, Sumatra
• Komodo

8 MALAYSIA
• Sipadan

9 MALDIVES

10 MEXICO
• Cabo Pulmo National Marine Park

11 SEYCHELLES
• Cousin Island

12 THAILAND
• Similan Islands (Nov–May)

13 USA
• Laniakea, Oahu, Hawaii

TOURS
www.aquatours.com
www.dive-the-world.com
www.diveworldwide.com

FIND OUT MORE
www.conserveturtles.org
www.seaturtle.org
www.turtles.org

✔ Swim slowly and calmly

 Touch a turtle or crowd them out

DIVING WITH
SHARKS

"*Using a reef hook, I'm **clinging** to a rock. The current is **so strong** that when I turn sideways it tries to tear my mask from my face. Above me, **dozens** of schooling hammerhead sharks **weave effortlessly** against this overwhelming force, shiny white bellies set against the deep-blue backdrop. Several veer off and head in my direction. My **heart is racing** – both from the effort needed to breathe in this whirlpool and the **sheer thrill**. Cold dark eyes, perched out wide, **gawk** at us. Then with barely a twist of their fins, they abruptly change direction to rejoin their hunting pack.*"

IAN WOOD

THE ENCOUNTER

People either love or hate sharks; there doesn't seem to be any middle ground. Yet nearly all of the fear stems from misconceptions; generally sharks are inherently shy of humans. Not that you can blame them; millions of sharks perish at the hands of people every year and this massacre is putting many species under severe strain. So the question is – are shark encounters dangerous? On average, about eight people are killed each year by sharks, with some attacks thought to occur when a surfer is mistaken for a seal. Putting this into some kind of context – over 700 people are killed annually by electric toasters, and 600 by falling off chairs.

There are over 350 species of shark, but white- and black-tip reef sharks are the most commonly encountered by divers and snorkellers on tropical reefs, and they'll usually give you a wide berth. Depending on where you dive, you could also see other species including nurse sharks, hammerheads, great whites,

ADDED BONUS

Other marine life converges in the currents that sweep by islands and rocky pinnacles, so tuna, shoals of snapper, jack fish and angry-looking trevally are all possibilities. But to encounter schooling barracuda is the ultimate: a tornado-like eddy of sheath-like silver fish, all suspended in the sea. Despite the horror stories, you can safely swim right inside the vortex, to be surrounded by hundreds of sets of fang-like teeth.

▲   Great white sharks are the largest predatory fish in the ocean.
◄◄   Schooling hammerhead sharks offer one of the most impressive underwater encounters.

leopard, tiger and bull sharks. If you are a shark fanatic and want to meet specific species, choose your dive sites with this in mind.

CAGE DIVING WITH GREAT WHITES

For an extremely close encounter with great white sharks, cage diving is the adrenalin-pumping activity. On board your boat, the crew will bait the water with a mixture of tuna, sardines and fish oil which soon attracts circling sharks. In wet suit and weighted jacket, you step off the side and into the cage for a spectacular view of the feeding frenzy. No diving experience is necessary – you breathe through tubes that rise up towards the boat, while the cage floats just beneath the surface. Typically these cages have space for four or five people, and you'll spend half an hour in the water. That's enough time to witness these ocean juggernauts, either cruising by or inquisitively eyeballing you from close quarters.

IN BRIEF

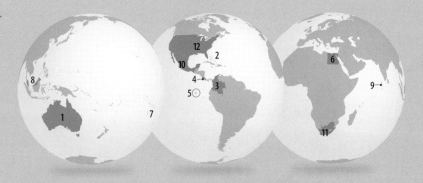

SIZE
Reef shark ave 1.5m/25kg; great white up to 6m/2,300kg

STATUS
From leopard shark, least concern; to black- & white-tip reef sharks, tiger shark, bull shark, near threatened

HOW
Diving, cage diving

WHO
Diving advanced divers 18+; cage diving 10+

WHEN
All year, unless specified

WHERE

1 AUSTRALIA
- Port Lincoln: great white (May–Oct)
- Great Barrier Reef, Neptune Islands, Osprey Reef: nurse, reef

2 BAHAMAS tiger, lemon

3 COLOMBIA
- Malpelo Island: hammerhead

4 COSTA RICA
- Cocos Island: hammerhead

5 ECUADOR
- Galápagos Islands: hammerhead

6 EGYPT
- Ras Mohammad, Elphinstone & Brothers: oceanic white-tip, hammerhead

7 FRENCH POLYNESIA
- Rangiroa: reef

8 MALAYSIA
- Sipadan: black- & white-tip
- Layang-layang: hammerhead (Mar–Aug)

9 MALDIVES black- & white-tip, grey nurse, tiger, leopard

10 MEXICO
- Guadalupe Island: great white (Aug–Oct)
- Socorro Islands: hammerhead (Nov–May)

11 SOUTH AFRICA
- Cape Point: great white

12 USA
- Farallon Islands: great white (Aug–Nov)

TOURS
www.diveworldwide.com
www.greatwhiteadventures.com
www.sharkdiver.com

FIND OUT MORE
www.bite-back.com
www.sharkalliance.org
www.sharktrust.org

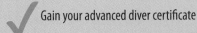 Gain your advanced diver certificate

 Be afraid

SNORKELLING & DIVING WITH
WHALE SHARKS

*"I'm standing on a boat, watching for **giant shadows** in the sea. When we spot one, **I slip overboard** and peer into the blue. Gliding just below the surface, propelled by **graceful** sweeps of its tail, the whale shark moves **closer**. Mottled markings on its back **twinkle** in the sun. It's only a few metres away now, **gaping mouth** sweeping up plankton, gills **quivering** on either side. I can see right inside – like looking down into a giant tube of flesh. The huge fish **stares** back at me through small dark eyes, completely out of proportion to its body size. But although **I'm dwarfed** by this animal, there is no fear – just a sense of **calm**."*

IAN WOOD

THE ENCOUNTER

Whale sharks spend quite a lot of time feeding near the surface so snorkelling affords easy access. Diving, however, offers the flexibility to go deeper and join them in their underwater world. Either way, there'll be plenty of direct eye contact.

There's an instant thrill when your skipper gives the command to slide into the sea: you're about to come face to face with the world's biggest fish. (Despite the name and the size – double the length of a great white shark – it's not a whale.) But this is the gentle giant of the ocean, extreme in size, but also in its diet. Whale sharks are filter feeders, surviving on tiny particles of plankton. You'll need to be a confident swimmer to keep up, but providing you respect their space – staying at least five metres away – they will happily let you swim along side, cavernous mouths guzzling plankton as they sail through the water. That said, although whale sharks are in themselves harmless, it's important to avoid swimming near their tail fins as these could crash on you with quite an impact.

WHALE SHARKS & CONSERVATION

The development of whale-shark tourism can create powerful economic incentives for conservation, but it's essential that basic guidelines are adhered to. If operators put too many guests on a boat it can become chaotic, with the fish being chased and harassed. It's better to find a smaller group, ideally of no more than four. If you

▲   The mottled markings on a whale shark's back are individual to that animal and are used for identification purposes.
◀◀   Feeding on plankton, whale sharks are the gentle giants of the oceans.

  MARINE

ADDED BONUS

If you're searching for whale sharks in the Gulf of Mexico you could be lucky and witness the mass migration of golden rays. Also known as cownose rays, they look like giant leaves floating just under the water's surface, with schools sometimes numbering several thousand individuals. But these aren't plankton feeders: they use their rows of flattened teeth like nutcrackers to feed on a variety of different shellfish.

have an underwater camera, upload your photos to the Ecocean whale-shark database (www.whaleshark.org). The patterns on their backs are unique to individual whale sharks, so scientists can use your photographs to determine where and when each individual has been spotted.

IN BRIEF

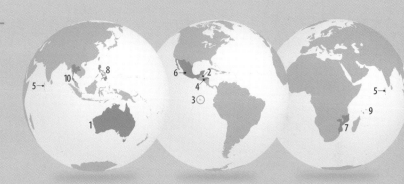

SIZE
Largest confirmed individual 12.65m/36,000kg

STATUS
Vulnerable

HOW
Diving & snorkelling

WHO
18+

WHEN & WHERE

1 AUSTRALIA
• Ningaloo Reef (Apr–Jul)

2 BELIZE
• Placencia (Mar–Jun)

3 ECUADOR
• Galápagos Islands (Jun–Sep)

4 HONDURAS
• Utila (Mar–Apr, Aug–Sep)

5 MALDIVES (Jul–Nov)

6 MEXICO
• Holbox Island (Jun–Sep)

7 MOZAMBIQUE
• Tofo (Sep–Dec)

8 PHILIPPINES
• Donsol Bay (Jan–Apr)

9 SEYCHELLES
• Mahe (Aug–Jan)

10 THAILAND
• Richelieu Rock & Hin Daeng (Apr–May)

TOURS
www.aqua-firma.co.uk
www.diveworldwide.com
www.donsolecotour.com
www.holboxwhalesharktours.com
www.whalesharkdive.com

FIND OUT MORE
www.marinemegafauna.org
www.whaleshark.org
www.whalesharkproject.org

 Give the whale shark plenty of space

 Get too close to its tail fin

DIVING WITH
MANTA RAYS

"*The only sound is my rhythmic breathing, bubbles rising up on every exhalation. I'm kneeling on the ocean floor. Ahead of me, three mantas glide above the reef – **five-metre wings**, swooping round in **mesmerising arcs**. Each orbit brings them closer, until they're almost overhead – white undercarriages backlit by the sun. Then one peels off and heads towards me, its gaping mouth scooping plankton in its path. Small bright eyes stare straight into mine, forging a connection that imbues **a deep sense of knowing**. Then it flies up and over – less than an arm's length away. There's the lightest of touches as its wingtip brushes my head; a caress of such **exquisite precision** that **I feel charmed**. Now it's somersaulting, over and over, until it soars away, rejoining its flying squadron.*"

IAN WOOD

Manta rays have the largest brain relative to body size of any fish.

THE ENCOUNTER

Prepare to be awestruck; diving with manta rays is like coming face to face with an other-worldly creature. No animal – even in the air – flies as majestically as this.

Mantas are inquisitive by nature and, providing you stay still, will often come extremely close. It's vital to follow some basic rules, though, both to maximise this meeting and for the well-being of the rays. Ask your dive operator how many people will be in your group (ideally six or fewer) and check that they give a proper briefing about how people should behave under water.

Typically, you'll see a small group of mantas – usually up to five, and often at a cleaning station. Rather than swimming over these areas, which could force the mantas to leave, stay down low and wait for them to approach you. Gradually they'll glide closer in circular patterns, until often they'll be near enough to touch. But keep your arms by your side – or folded in front – and let the interaction happen on their terms; never touch a manta ray.

BLAME THE TRAFFIC

Cleaning stations are small areas of reef that are critical for the well-being of manta rays, but on the more popular dive sites, there is concern that the increasing presence of divers is reducing the numbers of visiting mantas.

▲   Sharing the ocean with these graceful giants always induces a sense of wonder.

SPOTTED EAGLE RAYS

Spotted eagle rays are one of the most visually stunning creatures in the marine world, with signature patterns of white spots and rings dappled on their bluish dorsal surface. Smaller than mantas, they are diamond shaped with large wings tapered like a bird's, and a long venomous barbed tail trailing out behind. You'll either see a solitary eagle ray flying by a reef, or occasionally a squadron passing in formation, but don't expect them to come close; they're far less curious than their cousins

Rather like your regular trip to the dentist, mantas drop in so that cleaner fish such as wrasse can eat the parasites from their gill cavities. In southern Mozambique, scientists have found that the majority of visiting mantas have been victims of shark attacks, with an assortment of bites and wounds that the cleaner fish also help to heal.

IN BRIEF

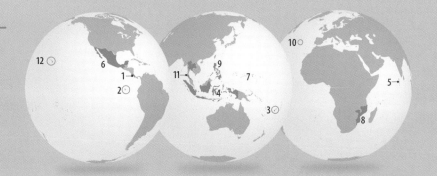

SIZE
Wingspan up to 7m/1,000kg

STATUS
Near threatened

HOW
Diving

WHO
18+

WHEN & WHERE

1 COSTA RICA
- Catalina Islands (Nov–May)

2 ECUADOR
- Galápagos Islands (Dec–May)

3 FIJI
- Kadavu (all year)

4 INDONESIA
- Kri Island, Papua (all year)
- Manta Point, Bali (all year)

5 MALDIVES (all year)

6 MEXICO
- Socorro Islands (Nov–May)

7 MICRONESIA
- Yap (Dec–Apr for greatest numbers)

8 MOZAMBIQUE
- Tofo (all year)

9 PHILIPPINES
- Donsol (Dec–May)

10 AZORES
- (Mar–Oct)

11 THAILAND
- Koh Bon (Nov–May)

12 USA
- Kona, Hawaii (all year)

TOURS
www.diveworldwide.com
www.diving-world.com
www.regal-diving.co.uk

FIND OUT MORE
www.mantarayconservation.org
www.mantaray-world.com
www.marinemegafauna.org

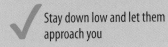 Stay down low and let them approach you

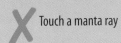 Touch a manta ray

THE WORLD OF THE
PUFFIN

"*Streamlined it isn't – in fact the puffin's **clumsy flapping** wings don't seem sufficient for the bloated undercarriage. Like a bizarre cross between a clown and a miniature cargo plane. But at the **last moment** it leans back, bright orange **legs splay** out wide, and in it comes, landing almost with a touch of style. Streaks of silver eels hang from its multi-coloured beak; red and black eye markings are set against a **pure white** face. It waddles across the ground – **ignoring me** as it passes barely two metres away – until it finds its burrow. Here, it's greeted by its partner and with a final **shuffle**, both disappear inside their earthy home.*"

IAN WOOD

THE ENCOUNTER

I challenge anyone surrounded by hundreds of puffins to keep a straight face. With a comical appearance and a wobbly slapstick walk, these are one of the most endearing of birds. During the breeding season, you'll be able to observe them much closer than many other birds, but it's important to keep a distance from their burrows (at least three metres away) or you risk disturbing them at this vital time.

Puffins spend most of their lives at sea, returning to land only to breed. Using their beaks to shovel soil, they dig a metre-long burrow, lined with feathers at the rear. Once it's excavated, they return to the same burrow every year, giving it a spring clean at the start of the season. Theirs is an equal partnership; while one partner keeps an eye on things at home, the other shambles out and prepares for take-off, whirring through the air before coming back with rows of sand eels clenched in its bill.

WEAR A HAT

Puffins share several of their breeding grounds with large numbers of Arctic terns. These fearless birds will do anything to protect their chicks and nests. Pre-emptive strikes seem to be the tactic of choice: swooping down, they will peck you on the head, sometimes leaving behind a smelly reminder of their attack.

▲   Puffins live on the open ocean for most of their lives, returning to land only once a year to breed.
◥   Thousands of gannets gather on Scotland's Bass Rock between February and October.
◀◀   With comical faces and ungainly bodies, puffins are one of the most endearing birds.

SEABIRD SANCTUARY

Wherever there are puffins, there'll be other birds such as guillemots, razorbills, shags, cormorants and oystercatchers, all out for their share of the fishy spoils. But on Scotland's Bass Rock, these are upstaged by the world's most concentrated population of gannets. Between February and October, over 100,000 cover this islet in a layer of white. As your boat approaches, crew members toss fish into the water, attracting a frenzy of activity: hundreds of birds diving in front of you, piercing the water at speeds of up to 100km/h. Groups of up to 12 people may land, but be warned. The stench of ammonia is so strong that it lingers in your mouth, and the noise — a pulsating, croaking sound — is almost overbearing. Gannets can be aggressive, fiercely protecting their nests, but if you approach extremely slowly you can observe from just a metre away as they lovingly entwine their elegant necks and weave in synchronisation, or engage in 'sky pointing' — when they strain their beaks towards the heavens, while raising alternate webbed feet off the ground.

IN BRIEF

PUFFIN SPECIES
Atlantic, horned & tufted puffins, & rhinoceros auklet

SIZE
Up to 30cm tall/500g

STATUS
Atlantic, horned, tufted, rhinoceros: least concern

HOW
Boat & on foot

WHO
No age limit

WHEN
May—Aug

WHERE

1 CANADA
• Witless Bay Ecological Reserve, Newfoundland

2 ICELAND
• Látrabjarg

3 IRELAND
• Skellig Islands

4 NORWAY
• Runde Island

5 UK
• Bass Rock
• Farne Islands
• Isle of May
• St Kilda
• Shetland Islands
• Skomer Island
• Treshnish Islands

6 USA
• Eastern Egg Rock, Maine
• Kenai Fjords National Park, Alaska

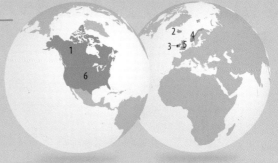

TOURS
www.farne-islands.com
www.seabird.org
www.shetlandtours.co.uk
www.turusmara.com

FIND OUT MORE
www.projectpuffin.org
www.seabird.org

 Take a hat

 Get too close to any nests

PICTURE CREDITS

Credits are listed in chronological order, specifying the position of the image on the page where necessary. For front and back cover credits, see page 2.

GLOSSARY OF SCIENTIFIC NAMES

albatross, waved *Phoebastria irrorata*
alligator, American *Alligator mississippiensis*
ant lion *Myrmeleon spp*
ant, leaf-cutter *Atta cephalotes*
anteater, giant *Myrmecophaga tridactyla*
armadillo *Dasypus spp*
auklet, rhinoceros *Cerorhinca monocerata*

baboon, gelada *Theropithecus gelada*
banner fish *Heniochus acuminatus*
barracuda *Sphyraena barracuda*
bear, black *Ursus americanus*
bear, Eurasian brown *Ursus arctos arctos*
bear, grizzly *Ursus arctos horribilis*
bear, polar *Ursus maritimus*
bear, skunk *Gulo gulo*
bear, sloth *Melursus ursinus*
boar, wild *Sus scrofa*
bonobo *Pan paniscus*
booby, blue-footed *Sula nebouxii*

caiman, yacare *Caiman yacare*
capybara *Hydrochoerus hydrochaeris*
cheetah *Acinonyx jubatus*
chestnut-eared araçari *Pteroglossus
    castanotis*
chimpanzee *Pan troglodytes*
clownfish *Amphiprion spp*
cockatoo, suphur-crested *Cacatua galerita*
condor, Andean *Vultur gryphus*
condor, California *Gymnogyps californianus*
crocodile, American *Crocodylus acutus*

dolphin, Atlantic spotted *Stenella frontalis*
dolphin, bottlenose *Tursiops truncates*
dolphin, Hector's dolphin
    Cephalorhynchus hectori
dolphin, spinner *Stenella longirostris*
drongo, fork-tailed *Dicrurus adsimilis*

eagle, bald *Haliaeetus leucocephalus*
elephant, African bush *Loxodonta africana*
elephant, African forest *Loxodonta cyclotis*
elephant, Asian *Elephas maximus*
elephant shrew *Elephantulus spp*

fox, Arctic *Alopex lagopus*
fox, crab-eating *Cerdocyon thous*
frigatebird, magnificent *Fregata magnificens*
fur seal, Antarctic *Arctocephalus gazella*
fur seal, Galápagos
    Arctocephalus galapagoensis

gannet, northern *Morus bassanus*
gibbon *Hylobates spp*
giraffe *Giraffa camelopardalis*
gorilla, mountain *Gorilla beringei beringei*
gorilla, western lowland *Gorilla gorilla gorilla*
gorillas, eastern lowland
    Gorilla beringei graueri

heron, purple *Ardea purpurea*
hippopotamus, common *Hippopotamus
    amphibius*
hippopotamus, pygmy *Choeropsis liberiensis*

ibis, white *Eudocimus albus*
iguana, marine *Amblyrhynchus cristatus*

jacana, African *Actophilornis africanus*
jaguar *Panthera onca*

kingfisher, malachite *Alcedo cristata*
kingfisher, woodland *Halcyon senegalensis*
Komodo dragon *Varanus komodoensis*

lammergeier (bearded vulture)
    Gypaetus barbatus
lemur, ring-tailed *Lemur catta*
lemur, Verreaux's sifaka *Propithecus verreauxi*
leopard *Panthera pardus*
leopard, snow *Panthera uncia*
lion *Panthera leo*
lynx *Lynx lynx*

macaque, Japanese *Macaca fuscata*
macaw, hyacinth
    Anodorhynchus hyacinthinus
manatee *Trichechus manatus latirostris*
mayfly, Tisza *Palingenia longicauda*
monkey, capuchin *Cebus spp*
monkey, golden *Cercopithecus kandti*
monkey, golden snub-nosed
    Rhinopithecus roxellana
monkey, howler *Alouatta spp*
monkey, proboscis *Nasalis larvatus*
monkey, red colobus *Procolobus badius*

ocelot *Leopardus pardalis*
orangutan (Borneo) *Pongo pygmaeus*
orangutan (Sumatra) *Pongo abelii*
otter, giant river *Pteronura brasiliensis*
owl, pygmy *Glaucidium spp*
oxpecker *Buphagus spp*

panda, giant *Ailuropoda melanoleuca*
panda, red *Ailurus fulgens*
parrotfish, bumphead
    Bolbometopon muricatum
penguin, Adélie *Pygoscelis adeliae*
penguin, African *Spheniscus demersus*
penguin, blue *Eudyptula minor*
penguin, emperor *Aptenodytes forsteri*
penguin, Galápagos *Spheniscus mendiculus*
praying mantis *Mantodea*
proboscis monkey *Nasalis larvatus*
puffin, Atlantic *Fratercula arctica*
puffin, horned *Fratercula corniculata*
puffin, tufted *Fratercula cirrhata*
puma *Puma concolor*

quetzal *Pharomachrus mocinno*

ray, giant manta *Manta birostris*
ray, golden (cow-nosed) *Rhinoptera
    steindachneri*
ray, reef manta *Manta alfredi*
ray, spotted eagle *Aetobatus narinari*
rhinoceros, African white *Ceratotherum
    simum*
rhinoceros, African black *Diceros bicornis*
rhinoceros beetle *Xyloryctes jamaicensis*

sea lion, Galápagos *Zalophus wollebaeki*
sea lion, South American *Otaria flavescens*
seal, grey *Halichoerus grypus*
seal, leopard *Hydrurga leptonyx*
shark, black-tip reef *Carcharhinus melanopterus*
shark, great white *Carcharodon carcharias*
shark, hammerhead *Sphyrnidae sphyrna*
shark, white-tip reef *Triaenodon obesus*
sheep, blue *Pseudosis nayaur szechuanensis*
shoebill *Balaeniceps rex*
sifaka, Verreaux's *Propithecus verreauxi*
spider, ladybird *Eresus cinnaberinus*

tapir, South American *Tapirus terrestris*
tern, Antarctic *Sterna vittata*
tern, Arctic *Sterna paradisaea*
tiger, Bengal *Panthera tigris tigris*
tiger, white *Panthera tigris tigris*
tiger, Siberian (Amur) *Panthera tigris altaica*
tortoise, Galápagos *Geochelone nigra*
toucan, toco *Ramphastos toco*
trevally, big-eye *Caranx sexfasciatus*
turtle, green *Chelonia mydas*
turtle, hawksbill *Eretmochelys imbricata*

vulture, bearded (lammergeier)
    Gypaetus barbatus
vulture, Cape griffon *Gyps coprotheres*
vulture, griffon *Gyps fulvus*

walrus *Odobenus rosmarus*
weevil, giraffe-necked *Trachelophorus giraffa*
whale, beluga *Delphinapterus leucas*
whale, humpback *Megaptera novaeangliae*
whale, killer *Orcinus orca*
whale, Minke *Balaenoptera acutorostrata*
whale shark *Rhincodon typus*
wildebeest *Connochaetes taurinus*
wolf, Ethiopian *Canis simensis*
wolf, grey *Canis lupus*
wolverine *Gulo gulo*

zebra *Equus quagga*

INDEX

Entries in **bold** refer to major encounters. Page numbers in *italic* indicate photographs.

Entries in **bold** refer to major encounters. Page numbers in *italic* indicate photographs.

Entries in **bold** refer to major encounters. Page numbers in *italic* indicate photographs.